ISBN: 978-90-823443-0-1

Published by Effectual Strategy Press, Doetinchem, Netherlands - www.effectualstrategy.com

Print and finishing by BoekenGilde, Enschede, Netherlands - www.boekengilde.nl

Design by Factor 12, Deventer, Netherlands - www.factor12.nl

# The Strategy Handbook

A practical and refreshing guide
for making strategy work

Part I. Strategy Generation

Jeroen Kraaijenbrink

# Contents

# 1 Motivation

This first chapter explains why this book was written, what you can expect, where the ideas in this book come from, and how you can use this book in different ways. Altogether, these four topics should give you a sense of the purpose and nature of this book.

## The challenge: Putting strategy into practice

This book was written with one purpose in mind: Supporting you in making strategy work. To achieve this, I wanted to write a practical handbook that you can use to generate and execute strategy yourself. Perhaps you still need some support after reading it, but the overall idea of this handbook is that it should be self-explanatory so that it can be used independently.

I thought I had to write this book because the way strategy is generated and executed in the average organization that I've seen is not particularly compelling. Or to say it in a less political manner, the majority of organizations have substantial problems with strategy generation and strategy execution. Often there either a) is no strategy, b) it isn't clear enough, or c) it doesn't get executed. In the first case, strategy just doesn't get on the organization's agenda. Such organizations are typically too involved with survival and with running their daily business to pay attention to strategy. In the second case, there is attention to strategy, but the organization isn't able to get beyond vague mission and vision statements, quantitative goals, or abstract formulations that are otherwise not actionable. And in the third case, strategy remains a paper vehicle of which only a small part ever gets executed. In either case, the result is that strategy is unsuccessful.

These are not just my own observations. Numerous studies in recent decades confirm that strategy generation and execution are cumbersome processes. Dependent on the exact design of the studies, astonishing failure rates of 70-90 % have been reported. This means that just one out of every three to ten strategies are successfully executed. Even though strategy is a complex matter, that is a pretty poor score. Typical problems that have been found in such studies are vague strategy, conflicting priorities, over-optimism, a lack of addressing market needs, mismatch with the organization, lacking guidelines for implementation, lack of commitment, and so on.

These problems with strategy generation and execution certainly do not occur due to a lack of strategy books. On the contrary, a quick search on Amazon.com reveals that there are already over a 100,000 books on strategy. So, could another book like this make any difference? I hope so and I have an optimistic belief that it could. To find out how, we need to see how this book tries to be different from existing books. Of course, I have not read all 100,000+ of them, so I might have missed something. However, from what I've seen, we can roughly divide the existing books into two categories: Broad strategy books and focused strategy books.

## "The majority of organizations have substantial problems with strategy generation and strategy execution."

Broad strategy books, such as strategy textbooks, typically try to cover the entire scope of strategy by offering a collection of tools. Some of these tools are known under acronyms such as PESTLE, SWOT, 5FF, 7S, VRIO, 4P, BCG, or BSC. These tools are useful and the books are too. They support strategic analysis and making generic choices. But they hardly facilitate designing and developing concrete new strategy that can be executed. So they are quite good at telling you *what* you should pay attention to when generating and executing strategy. However, they don't give much guidance as to *how* to do it. Thus, although not entirely *im*practical, they are not practical enough.

On the other hand, there are focused books that are quite valuable too and often more practical. Such books typically try to make a specific point and a focused contribution to existing strategy approaches. I want to name four specifically, since they have been a great source of inspiration for me while writing this book: Chan Kim and Renée Mauborgne's *Blue Ocean Strategy*, Alexander Osterwalder and Yves Pigneur's *Business Model Generation*, Saras Sarasvathy's *Effectuation*, and Eric Ries's *The Lean Startup*. These four are all inspirational and practical books on strategy and entrepreneurship that provide new and different insights into how to generate new strategy. However, they offer partial solutions, not complete strategy approaches.

Thus, we have rather complete but not so practical strategy books on the one side, and rather practical but not so complete strategy books on the other. In order to be successful in practice though, you need both. Therefore, in this book, I have tried to take the best of both worlds and turn that into a practical strategy handbook that outlines a practical approach to strategy.

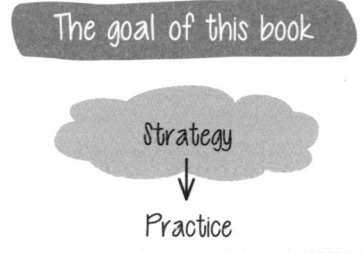

## Recipe for a handbook?

But what should a practical strategy handbook look like? For one thing, it needs to put strategy back on earth. If we look at how it is treated by textbooks, MBA programs, scholars, consultants, and organizations generally, strategy is often put too much on a pedestal. It seems some sort of mystical and elite boardroom thing that is made bigger than it actually is. Of course strategy is extremely important for organizations. However, as I hope to show you in this book, strategy can also be approached in a practical, down-to-earth manner.

A strategy handbook also needs to be rather complete without becoming bulky. If we want to foster successful strategy generation and execution, we have to make sure that all important steps and elements of strategy are covered. This means that this book does not just cover strategic analysis and decision-making, but also less honorable tasks such as turning strategy into a communicable message and getting people to actively work on strategy in the first place. It also means that a strategy handbook should cover strategy generation *and* strategy execution. Therefore, the book you are reading now is the first part of a series of handbooks. There will also be a second part on strategy execution. As I will briefly discuss in Chapter 2, strategy generation and execution are inextricably linked in practice and both are needed for successful strategy. I found it more practical though, to discuss them in two separate books. At any particular point in time you might only be interested in one of them. And if combined, the printed book would be about twice the size as it has now, which would make it pretty inconvenient to carry – and therefore less practical.

## "A strategy handbook needs to put strategy back on earth."

Since strategy is a complicated matter, a handbook should also be structured and thorough. On the one hand it should provide you with a clear step-by-step approach that guides you through the strategy process and makes sure that you don't skip essential steps. In order to remain practical, this approach needs to be as clear and simple as possible. On the other hand, exactly because strategy is a complicated matter, there is no use in dumbing things down. Strategy is simply difficult and you won't benefit from this handbook if it pretended strategy was easy. Therefore this book aims at balancing simplicity and depth.

A strategy handbook also needs to be concrete and hands-on. Concrete means that it has to descend from high-level mission and vision statements and from generic strategies and objectives towards the concrete elements of which strategy is composed. Only in that way can we make sure that we actually understand what is meant by strategy and assess whether it is good or not. Hands-on means that it provides you with information and tools that you can immediately apply in your own situation. In other words, it means that a handbook should be action-oriented and stimulates *doing* strategy rather than just thinking and talking about it. From Chapter 2 on you will see how this has been incorporated in this book.

Finally, a practical strategy handbook needs to be realistic as well. I certainly don't mean that it should limit your ambition and creativity and narrow down strategizing to small incremental changes. On the contrary, a strategy handbook should foster creativity and push you to come up with radically new ideas that go beyond the status quo. What I mean though, is that it should not ignore what is already there. Even in startups, but especially in existing organizations, there always is a current strategy that is lived by the organization and its people today. Whether we want it or not, this current strategy will have a large impact on any future strategy. This means that a strategy handbook has to embrace it and give it a proper place.

## Origins and methodological basis

Maybe you have read other strategy books. Quite a few of them – especially the ones that you find at airports and in local bookstores – are based on a set of in-depth case studies of several large, successful (and often US-based) firms. These books typically present 8-10 key rules of thumb supported with examples that tell you the do's and don'ts of strategy.

"This book draws on the vast body of literature on strategy and on my own experience."

That is interesting and useful, but this book has a slightly different basis. Rather than drawing on few case studies, it draws primarily on the vast body of knowledge on strategy that has been published over the past few decades. Because this covers thousands of case studies and incorporates the ideas of hundreds of intelligent authors, I thought this would be a more reliable basis than adding another set of case studies. And as it turns out, this body of knowledge is quite rich and useful.

The book also draws on my own experience. The strategy generation process and tools presented in this book have been developed on a trial-and-error basis with clients, executive students, and seminar participants. Furthermore, wherever possible I've applied them to my own business as well. So, much of what I preach in this book, I practice too. For those of you who are interested, the following few pages give a more detailed account of the journey that has led to this book.

## The start: Dissatisfaction, enthusiasm, and mismatches

The journey started with, on the one hand, dissatisfaction with some of the most widely-used strategy tools, in particular the SWOT analysis. As yearly studies by some of the big consultancy firms show, this is still amongst the most used strategy tools. As a tool though, its usefulness is limited because it is highly abstract and subjective and because it barely provides people with any real structure that helps them. The same, but to a lesser degree, applies also to other frequently used tools such as Michael Porter's 'five forces framework' and Michael Treacy and Fred Wiersema's 'value disciplines'. Although useful, my feeling was that it was possible and necessary to come up with something more practical and concrete than that.

> "It took six major versions and interactions with executives, managers, and entrepreneurs of about three hundred organizations."

On the other hand, I came across Alexander Osterwalder's PhD thesis and his 'business model canvas' (BMC) about five years ago. This canvas breaks down an organization's business model into its key elements and puts these together on a single sheet of paper, thereby providing a nice overview of what to pay attention to. This ingenious tool really helped companies innovate their own business models. So, I enthusiastically adopted it in my own teaching, training, and consulting activities, which worked quite well for a while.

When using the BMC more often though I started experiencing some limitations. I noticed that anything that was not mentioned in the BMC tended to be forgotten or ignored by people that use it. While Osterwalder and Pigneur's accompanying 'Business Model Generation' book pays attention to, for example, competition, this moved to the background when using the BMC because it was not covered in the canvas itself. Thus, people tended to exclusively focus on what was covered by the BMC. This is quite natural, and any model has this focusing effect: It draws attention to some factors, thereby moving attention away from other factors. However, if the attention is drawn away from key elements of strategy – such as competition – this is a problem. My conclusion was therefore that everything that is of crucial importance for strategy should be part of the same tool.

Also, when comparing the BMC to the strategy literature, there were some mismatches. Why, for example does the BMC pay explicit attention to customer relationships and channels, while this is not a central element in the strategy literature? Or, why doesn't the Business Model Generation book talk at all about an organization's mission, vision, and values, while these are essential elements of strategy? As I couldn't find satisfying answers to these questions, I concluded that a better tool was needed.

## The next step: Harvesting published insights

As a next step, I started gathering ideas from the existing literature for what an improved model and strategy approach should look like. In doing so, I combined insights from:

1. The traditional strategy literature. Dating back more than a century (some would even argue 2500 years) and growing exponentially over the past few decades, this literature provides in-depth insights into what strategy is, where it comes from, and what the important factors to consider are.
2. Recent approaches to strategy, business model generation, and design thinking. I reviewed, for example, alternatives for the BMC such as the 'lean canvas' and other design-oriented strategy tools and books.
3. Recent approaches to entrepreneurship, including 'effectuation', 'bricolage', and the 'lean startup' approach that reveal how experienced and successful entrepreneurs work.

All in all, I've read about two thousand books and academic papers on these topics over the past fifteen years. This, I thought, would form a reasonable starting point for developing a practical model and approach to strategy.

## The actual work: Design, trial, and error

Based on the first two phases I developed a first version of an alternative model to the BMC. This version was used in a couple of workshops with entrepreneurs, quickly leading to the conclusion that it wasn't the great improvement I had hoped for and that I needed to go back to the drawing board. Consequently, I made adjustments, made a new version, tried it out in practice again, revised, and so on and so forth. In a period of about three years various versions were tested in this way by:

- Discussing it in training sessions and executive MBA lectures with managers and entrepreneurs.
- Asking experts from practice and academia for feedback and suggestions.
- Blogging about the various versions and collecting online and offline responses.
- Applying it in workshops and consulting activities with managers and entrepreneurs.

Altogether it took six major versions and interactions with executives, managers, and entrepreneurs from about three hundred organizations before the final tool was ready. I then labeled it the *Strategy Sketch*, about which you will read more in Chapter 2.

These interactions also taught me a lot about how the Strategy Sketch could and should be used in practice. This provided me with further inputs for what the strategy generation process should look like and what kind of tools would be useful to support it. This crystallized into the five-step approach that this book is shaped around. Finally, several scholars and practitioners have read earlier versions of this book and provided me with extremely helpful feedback and suggestions.

# Four ways to use this book

Of course it is completely up to you how you use this book. You might read it page by page and from cover to cover. However, when actually using it as a handbook, I guess you also might want to skip parts, or move back and forth between different parts of the book. To guide you a little I have anticipated four ways of using this book. These four ways vary in the extent to which they actively make use of the process and content that are provided.

## 1 Checklist approach

The lightest of all four, the first approach is to use the book as a checklist to make sure that you pay attention to all the elements of strategy and all the steps of strategy generation. You might want to follow this approach when you are already knowledgeable about strategy and basically know how to generate it successfully. If you aim for this approach, you can immediately jump to the sections 'The ten elements of strategy' and 'The five steps of strategy generation' in Chapter 2 (pages 20 and 30).

## 2 Fast and frugal approach

The fast and frugal approach covers the core ideas of this book in a quick way. If you want minimum efforts, and to see some results, I suggest using this approach. For this you could use the following two parts of the book in addition to the two sections above:

- Chapter 4 (Mapping strategy). Based on the main tool of this book, the Strategy Sketch, it contains a set of questions, exercises, and inspirational checklists that you can use to quickly understand your current strategy and innovate it.
- The 'Stepping back for a moment' section on page 110. This section outlines a simple fast and frugal format you can use for strategy generation and that fits the structure of Chapter 4.

## "You might want to skip parts, or move back and forth between different parts of the book."

## 3 Systematic approach

You may also prefer a more systematic approach during which you go through a step-by-step process and reach more depth than with the fast and frugal approach. By following the systematic approach you make sure that you don't skip important parts of the strategy generation process. In this case, I suggest using the following parts of the book in addition to the parts mentioned above:

- Chapters 3 through 7, which present the five key steps of the strategy generation process: activating, mapping, assessing, innovating, and formulating strategy. Each of these chapters contains a variety of tools and tricks to guide you through the entire strategy generation process. You might want to focus on the questions, exercises, inspirational checklists, and examples, but skip the 'useful models' sections.

- Chapter 8 (Strategy generation formats), which presents five formats that can be used for strategy generation. Instead of the fast and frugal format, you could also use one or more of the other formats suggested there.

## 4 Unabridged approach

The most comprehensive way of using this book is the unabridged approach. With this approach you read the entire book carefully and use as much of it as possible during the strategy generation process. There are three reasons why you may want to do this. First, it is the best guarantee that you will be successful in generating new strategy. The effort is larger than with the other approaches, but so should be the pay-off. So, if you aim for maximum results, this is your approach. The second reason for following this approach is that it helps you in building up your own strategy expertise. By reading all the chapters and going through all the tools – including the 'useful models' sections – you can develop a deeper understanding of strategy generation. And third, reading the entire book increases the chance that you stumble upon something that you find particularly interesting or useful.

Whatever approach you choose, I wish you all the best in your strategy generation efforts! So, let's get started.

# 2 Getting ready

Whereas the first chapter has mainly given you some background to this book, this second chapter prepares you for the actual work. It defines and explains what strategy is and what the strategy generation process looks like. Also, to help you translate the ideas of his book into your own practice, the chapter introduces you to the four examples that will be used throughout this book, and shows you the mindset needed for effective strategy generation.

## Defining Strategy

An important thing to know upfront is that this book is mostly about what is called 'business level strategy'. Business level strategy is strategy at the level of business units and small to medium-sized firms. Typically it concerns organizations with a limited portfolio of products and services and that are run as single businesses. 'Corporate level strategy,' on the other hand, is strategy for larger organizations with multiple business units or divisions. Although important too, corporate level strategy is not covered in this part of the handbook. So, keep in mind that, whenever I use the word 'strategy,' I refer to business level strategy. Let's now turn to the meaning of that word.

"Stripped down to its essence, a strategy is a unique way of sustainable value creation."

There are almost as many definitions of strategy as there are people writing about it. Some focus on long-term planning, others on differentiating the organization from its competitors, and still others on an organization's actual decisions and actions. That there isn't a universal agreed-upon definition of strategy doesn't really matter. However, I should be clear about what is meant by strategy in this book because it has a substantial impact on how you generate and execute it.

I will start by providing a short definition of strategy. This provides you with an idea of the role and purpose of strategy. Then, in the next section, I will move on by presenting the elements strategy is made up of. This is needed to make sure that we actually understand and are talking about the same thing when we use the word strategy.

## A short definition of strategy

Stripped down to its essence, a strategy is *a unique way of sustainable value creation.* So, if we ask someone what the strategy of their organization is, we ask them about the organization's unique way of sustainable value creation. To understand what this means, let's look part by part at this definition.

**Value creation**
Strategy aims at creating something that has value and that matters to at least a number of people or organizations. This means that a strategy expresses what value an organization has and for whom. Organizations primarily create value through their products and services. This is what they produce, and as such this can be seen as their main reason of existence. Therefore, value creation is about the value an organization creates through its products and services.

Customers buy these products or services because they fulfill a particular need or desire. And since customers may buy them for very different reasons, value is subjective. People may buy a watch, for example, for very different reasons: Because it tells the time, because it is beautiful, or because it is expensive. This means that there is no absolute way of saying that something is valuable or an absolute way of measuring it. Of course, we can see the price of products and services, but this is not the same as their actual value for a specific customer. Furthermore, people may strongly disagree about what is valuable and what not. Because of this subjectivity, a strategy needs to express for whom value is created.

**Sustainable**
Strategy aims at value creation that is sustainable over time. This implies first that a strategy should be hard to copy or circumvent by others. Protection by patents might be the first thing you think about, but there are other ways as well. Think of, for example, secrecy, or having a unique and hard-to-imitate network.

Second, sustainable also means that an organization receives something in return for the value it creates. Usually this is money – if no one pays for the value that is created, an organization will have a hard time to sustain itself. It can also be information or other goods, though. Think about, for example, Facebook or Google, which are 'free' because you provide personal information in exchange for their products.

Third, to be sustainable a strategy also shouldn't rely too much on resources that are easily depleted. There is a touch of ethics because we could argue that organizations *ought to* make sure that they don't exhaust their resources. However, there is a practical component too: If a strategy relies on resources that are soon gone, this strategy cannot be sustained.

Finally, to be sustainable, a strategy should take into account the interests of important stakeholders. These are the people or organizations that influence your organization or are influenced by it. Examples are customers, suppliers, or interest groups. From an ethical point of view you could argue that organizations ought to take responsibility for their stakeholders because that is a good thing to do. However, also more practically this is a good idea, because if your strategy doesn't take care of your important stakeholders, it will be hard to sustain.

### Unique
A good strategy aims at doing something different from others. This doesn't have to be 100 % unique, but it should have at least some unique elements. This uniqueness may come from anywhere. You can think of, for example, your location, the specific history of the organization, or the friendliness of your employees. Uniqueness is so important because without it you cannot distinguish yourself from others. And if you want to compete with them, or convince customers to buy your products or services, you need to be able to tell what is special about you.

### Way
Strategy is not a fixed product, a set of goals, or a long-term plan that remains stable over time. Neither is it a statement or a slogan, or limited to what is written down in official documents. All of that we could call an organization's *explicit* strategy – the strategy as it is officially communicated. But that is not an organization's true strategy.

19

An organization's true strategy appears more implicitly in what it does; in its processes, actions, and routines. That strategy is an ongoing and active process that is lived by the organization on a daily basis. Thus, much more than a piece of text, strategy is a way of doing something – a unique way of sustainable value creation.

"An organization's true strategy appears implicitly in what it does; in its processes, actions, and routines."

## The ten elements of strategy

The above definition helps us to get at the essence of strategy and what it aims for. This is important, as it makes clear what strategy is and why we should bother about it in the first place. For actually working on your strategy, though, this definition is too abstract. To see how an organization can offer a unique way of sustainable value creation, we need to look more in depth at the elements strategy is made up of. A reading of the strategy literature and feedback during the writing process revealed ten core elements of strategy. Throughout this book I will frequently refer to these ten elements. In brief, they comprise the following:

1 Resources & competences. *What you have, what you are good at, and what makes you unique.*

Your resources and competences reflect what kind of unique means your organization has and what it is capable of. Resources are the things that you *have*, such as machines, people, information, location, money, and so on. Competences are the things you *can do*. These are the skills, capabilities, and processes you're good at. Together, these means determine to a large extent what kind of products and services an organization can offer.

2 Partners. *Whom you work with and who makes your products or services more valuable.*

Not only are your own resources and competences important for your strategy; also are those of the organizations and people you work with. Think of, for example, suppliers, universities, logistics services, or any other type of organization that could support you in offering something unique. Also, think of your or other people's personal networks, since these can give you access to valuable information or other means that the organization doesn't have.

3 Customers & needs. *The organizations and people you serve and which needs of them you fulfill.*

Obviously no organization can do without customers. Therefore, a strategy needs to specify who they are and what needs they have. To do this properly you do so on two levels. On the surface level you specify the kind of organizations or people you are targeting and which of their needs you are trying to fulfill. On a deeper level, you are also looking at the specific people that are involved. Think of those who *use* the product, those that *pay* for it, the people *deciding* about it, and those who *influence* and initiate that decision. They are all your customers and all their needs are relevant.

"A reading of the strategy literature and feedback during the writing process revealed ten core elements of strategy."

4 Competitors. *Others that your customers will compare you to in deciding whether or not to buy your products or services.*

Partners are the ones you work *with* and customers are the ones you work *for*. Competitors, on the other hand, are those people and organizations you work *against*. While you don't necessarily need to fight them aggressively, you have to deal with them somehow, if only because your customers can only spend their money once and compare you to them. Your competitors obviously include those organizations that do something similar to your organization. But don't forget substitutes or potential future competitors that might enter your industry soon. You are competing with them as well.

5 Value proposition. *What products and services you offer, how you offer them, and what added value they have for the customer.*

Your resources and competences and your partners determine what value you *can* create. Your customer and needs and your competitors, on the other hand, tell you what value you *should* create. With these inputs we can now move on to the core element of your strategy: Your value proposition. A good value proposition consists of three closely connected parts: 1) the *products or services* that you offer, 2) the *way* you get them to the customer, and 3) what they do to create *value* for the customer.

6 Revenue model. *What you receive in return for your offer, from whom, how, and when.*

When you create value you probably also want to get something in return. This is reflected in the sixth element of strategy, your revenue model. In plain terms, your revenue model shows how your organization makes money. A good revenue model explains *who pays* (this could be people other than your customers, such as a sponsor), *for what* (for example, for owning the product or for just using it), *how much* (the price level), and *how* (such as paying in advance or a subscription). Don't take payment too literally here. As we saw in the definition of 'sustainable' on page 18, it can also consist of information or any other type of goods.

7 Risks & costs. *What financial, social, and other risks and costs your bear and how you manage these.*

No strategy comes for free. Good strategy, therefore, makes clear what costs and risks there are and how the organization deals with them. Costs can be predicted and controlled quite well. They include financial but also other costs such as time, effort, pollution, or social effects. Risks, on the other hand, cannot be easily predicted or controlled. They reflect the bad things that could happen as a result of your strategy. Think of product risks, safety risks, technological risks, or financial risks.

**8** Values & goals. *What you want, where you want to go and what you find important.*

Together, the first five elements explain how your organization creates value and the sixth and seventh element reflect what you get in return. These cover an important share of your strategy. However, these elements don't say anything about the organization itself yet. For that reason, we need two further elements that represent your organization's identity. The first are your values and goals. These indicate what is important and desirable for the organization. To make this clear it is useful to make a distinction between the *vision* (the aspirations or dreams for the future), the mission (what kind of organization it should be on your journey towards this vision), *key values* (what is important), and *objectives* (what you want to achieve concretely).

**9** Organizational climate. *What your culture and structure look like and what is special about them.*

The second part of your identity is the organizational 'climate.' This covers the structure and culture of the organization. The organizational *structure* is the way tasks are divided and coordinated. Think of the organization's chart, job descriptions, and the way things are communicated. The organizational *culture*, on the other hand, reflects the attitudes and behaviors that are characteristic of the organization. You find it in, for example, the organization's symbols, dress code, stories, or habits. The organizational climate is important for your strategy because it can be an important enabler or barrier. An innovative 'boutique' strategy, for example, asks for quite a different climate than a large-volume, low-cost strategy.

**10** Trends & uncertainties. *What happens around you that affects your organization and what uncertainties you face.*

The tenth and last element of strategy concerns the relevant trends and uncertainties that are happening in the direct or broader environment of your organization. *Trends* are changes in your environment that are relatively clear and inevitable and that you will somehow have to deal with. You might think of increased automation or a shrinking market. *Uncertainties* are the changes in your environment that you don't know the outcome of yet. Think of,

23

for example, a new law that might or might not be passed and that will have a direct impact on your strategy.

## The ten elements in a picture: The Strategy Sketch

With ten elements, this is quite a list. But now you have all the key elements of strategy. Together, these ten elements give a much more detailed and concrete idea of the meaning of the term strategy than the definition gave. As a list though, it might look still somewhat unstructured. Therefore, inspired by the Business Model Canvas, I've developed a visual tool that combines the ten elements in a structured and coherent way and that will be used throughout this book: *The Strategy Sketch*.

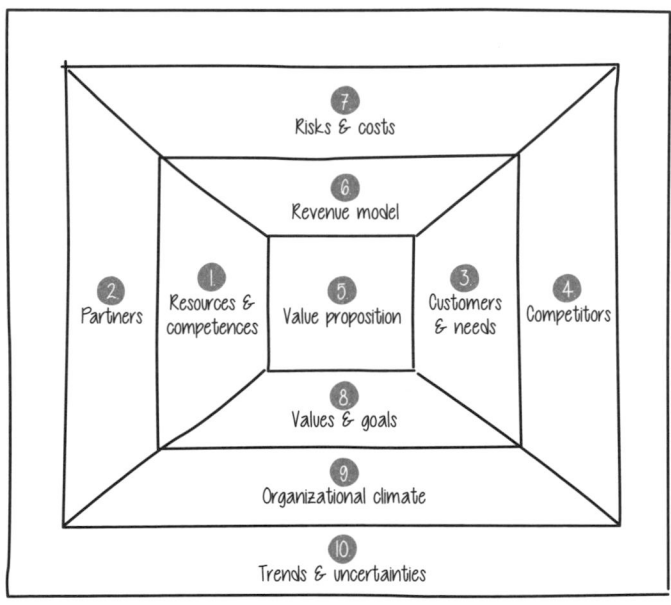

The Strategy Sketch

On the left-hand side of the Strategy Sketch we find the organization's *means* – its resources and competences and its partners. These tell you what value the organization is able to offer. On the other side we find the organization's *market* – its customers and needs and its competitors. These show you the kind of value that is being asked for. Together with strategy's core element – the value proposition, these elements show how the organization creates value.

## "The Strategy Sketch: A visual tool that combines the ten elements of strategy in a structured and coherent way."

Above the value proposition we see what the organization gets in return for the value it creates through its combination of revenue model and risks and costs. Below the value proposition we find the organization that is doing all of this and that drives and supports the value proposition – represented by its values and goals and its organizational climate.

Finally, around these nine elements we find the trends and uncertainties that form the wider context of the organization.

## Defining strategy generation

Now we have seen what strategy is and what it is composed of, we can move on to defining strategy generation (this section) and discussing the steps it is made up of (next section). I will start by discussing the relationship between strategy generation and execution and then move on to discussing the three key features of strategy generation.

### The relation between strategy generation and strategy execution

Strategy generation and strategy execution are two intertwined but quite different processes. Both are needed for a strategy to be successful, but they are also distinct. Simply put, strategy generation is about *developing ideas* and strategy execution is about *realizing* those ideas.

The most common way of seeing the relationship between them is to present them as two sequential stages in a process: You generate strategy first, and than execute it. While this is intuitive and easy to understand, I find it more useful to see strategy generation and strategy execution as two parallel processes (see the figure below). Strategy generation is a *conceptual* process in which strategy is thought up, imagined, talked about, etc. Strategy at this level exists in people's minds, and in words and pictures that can be shared. Strategy execution, on the other hand, is a process in which strategy is actually *realized* through people's actions and by doing something with 'stuff' – technology, materials, buildings, etc.

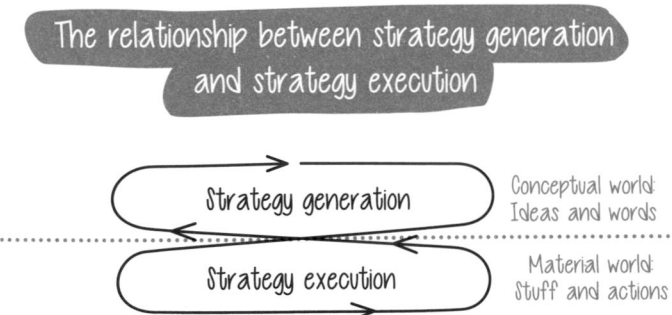

The relationship between strategy generation and strategy execution

Strategy generation and execution influence one another. This is important because it means that not does only strategy generation influence strategy execution, but also the other way around. Of course, strategy generation may come before strategy execution, and your organization might separate them definitively into two stages. However, it is also possible that strategy execution precedes strategy generation – you might do something first and only later think about it and learn from it. And even if strategy execution comes formally after strategy generation in your organization, it still influences strategy generation: You will usually somehow take into account whether the strategy you generate can also be executed.

**Key features of strategy generation**

When you engage in strategy generation, it is good to understand what kind of process you're getting yourself into. This gives you an idea of the kind of activities you will be primarily doing. From

# "Strategy generation and strategy execution are two intertwined but quite different processes."

reading the average strategy textbook, you might get the idea that strategy generation is primarily an analytical and rational process. Strategy generation as it is presented there typically relies heavily on information gathering, thorough analysis, systematic decision-making, and careful planning. If we want strategy generation to be practical though, we also need to take into account that strategy generation is a *creative*, *interactive*, and *emergent* process.

**Strategy generation is creative**
A first key feature of strategy generation is that it is a creative process. This means that it is about using your imagination, intuition, and judgment to come up with original insights and ideas. So, you shouldn't over-rely on 'objective' information and 'rational' analysis, but combine this with a good dose of your own and others' individual and subjective input. Since your competitors probably have access to the same 'objective' information and use the same kind of 'rational' analysis, only in this way can you expect to come up with something unique that is different from what they will be doing.

That strategy generation is creative also means that it is a process in which you *create* new things that weren't there before. This includes creating new products, services, customers, markets, and even creating (or at least influencing) your broader environment. Rather than making yourself over-dependent on your environment, try not taking it too seriously. Next to analyzing it, also try to influence it and focus on those actions that are within your own control rather than those depending on where the environment might or might not go. This is often more useful than relying on some market research that might tell you whether there is a demand for your product or not. Expert entrepreneurs work this way, so why shouldn't you?

Finally, 'creative' also means that you should try to have some fun during the strategy generation process. Of course, strategy is a serious matter with serious consequences for your organization. But if you can have some fun during this process it will not only lead to a nicer process, but also to better outcomes, as having fun boosts your creativity and increases your chances of better outcomes.

### Strategy generation is interactive

If done well, strategy generation is an interactive process. From traditional books on strategy you might get the idea that you can strategize effectively by locking a few people up in a room with some models and a lot of information. I haven't seen this work very often or very well. If you want to be more successful, you should make your strategy generation process more interactive. So, instead of relying on 'hard' paper-based information, you might want to see the people around you as your main sources of information. They have worked for the organization for a while and maybe even much longer in the industry, so you can assume that they actually know quite a lot about it.

Making strategy generation interactive has two main advantages. First, by including a variety of people from inside and outside the organization you get more variety and perspectives. More variety alone increases the chance of a good idea that really takes you beyond the status quo. Second, including them also makes it much more likely that they will be committed to the strategy being generated. This promotes successful execution.

It is important to include people from within your organization (managers, staff, or other employees) and from outside (particularly customers and suppliers). After all, you need them to turn your strategy into practice, so why not include them early on? It can also help to deliberately include people that are critical, or of which you know they might have a very deviating view. Again, this increases variety and thereby the chance that you come up with unique and new ideas.

### Strategy generation is emergent

Strategy generation is also an emergent process. This means that it doesn't follow a strict linear step-by-step logic and that it usually leads you to a different place than you originally anticipated. So, although you might plan to go from A to B in a more or less straight line following the plan, the reality is that you might end up at place E because B doesn't exist, C didn't work out, or you stumbled unexpectedly at D. Since E could be a much better place than B (which in this case it certainly is because B doesn't exist), it is generally a good idea to embrace unexpected twists rather than systematically avoiding them.

Another way in which strategy generation is emergent is that it requires some trial and error. This doesn't mean you should just blindly try something new and see what happens. It means that rather than only trying to predict upfront what will happen or what customers will need, you should also test your ideas in practice and learn from that. Based on what you learn you will then redirect and adjust your initial strategy.

# "Strategy generation is as much about making adjustments and letting things go than about starting something new."

The fact that strategy generation is emergent also means that it is an ongoing process. Both strategy generation and strategy execution run the entire lifetime of an organization. This means that whatever new strategy you develop, there is usually a large part of the organization and the strategy that doesn't change and that follows a path that was set out before. This is important, as it means that strategy generation is as much about making adjustments and letting things go than about starting something new. This is depicted in the following picture, which shows how strategy changes as a result of new ideas coming in and old ideas leaving:

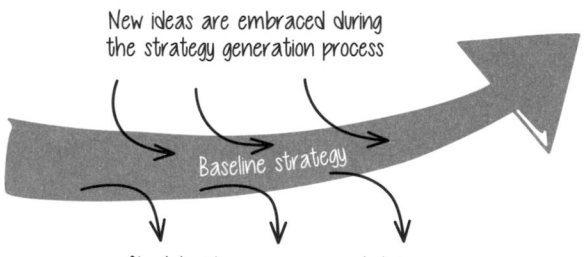

Strategy as an emergent process

New ideas are embraced during the strategy generation process

Baseline strategy

Obsolete ideas are removed during the strategy generation process

# The five steps of strategy generation

Having seen some of the key characteristics of strategy generation, we can now move on to have a more detailed look at the steps it is made up of. From the literature and interactions with entrepreneurs, managers, and executives, I have extracted five key steps that cover the entire strategy generation process. As you can infer from the table of contents, these five steps form the core of this book. I briefly summarize them below.

**Step 1**    Activating key stakeholders. *Making key persons in the organization receptive to new strategy and mobilizing the resources needed for strategy generation.*

At this first step, you make your organization ready for new strategy so that the strategy generation process is not doomed to fail before it actually starts. An important reason for strategic failure is that organizations don't pay sufficient attention to strategy. They are so invested in strategy execution that they fail to engage in strategy generation on time or with sufficient drive and ambition. In this case, strategy generation needs to start with making the organization strategically active and getting it from strategy execution mode into a strategy generation mode. Obviously, if your 'organization' is just you, or if people are already convinced, you can skip this step. In all other cases, though, it is crucial.

**Step 2**    Mapping strategy. *Identifying the organization's strategy by describing it on the basis of its ten core elements.*

At this step you develop an understanding of the organization's strategy by mapping it onto all ten elements of the Strategy Sketch. This is not so much about mapping the formal strategy that has been written down, but about mapping the actual and more detailed strategy as it is experienced by the organization. This step is not only important for existing organizations, but also for startups. Even there, for instance, there can be particular resources and competences or ideas about customers and competitors that can be taken as a starting point. This step is pertinently not meant to restrict strategy generation to what is already there or to small incremental changes.

However, without a proper understanding of the organization's actual strategy, it is quite hard to really innovate or improve it.

Step 3  Assessing strategy. *Judging and testing the quality of the organization's strategy against relevant criteria.*

At this third step, you assess your strategy in order to diagnose its quality and to identify its strengths and weaknesses. So, at this step you judge and test how good your strategy is and where it can or should be improved. This step serves two roles. First, it can be an assessment of your current strategy. As such, this step is a good starting point for revealing how your strategy could be improved at the next step. Second, it can also be an assessment of your newly generated strategy. As such, it serves as a judgment of the quality of the new strategy and its chances for success.

Step 4  Innovating strategy. *Renewing and redesigning the organization's strategy through incremental or radical innovation.*

At this fourth step you start the actual generation of new strategy. Based on the existing strategy, explicitly deviating from it, or starting from scratch, this step focuses on generating new, innovative ideas for your strategy. As such, it is probably the most creative step of the strategy generation process. Next to developing new ideas, this step also explicitly looks at what parts of your existing strategy should be kept and what parts should be left behind.

Step 5  Formulating strategy. *Capturing the organization's strategy in words and pictures that can be understood by the target audience.*

At this last step you turn your strategy into a form that can be communicated to others. This is an essential step, as a strategy can only be really effective if it can be formulated in a clear and comprehensible manner. This last step forms a temporary closure of the strategy generation process. As explained above, strategy generation and execution are ongoing processes that are inextricably linked. However, at some point in time, you need to stop generating new ideas and focus on their execution. As such, this fifth step brings the attention back to where Step 1 drew it away: Strategy execution.

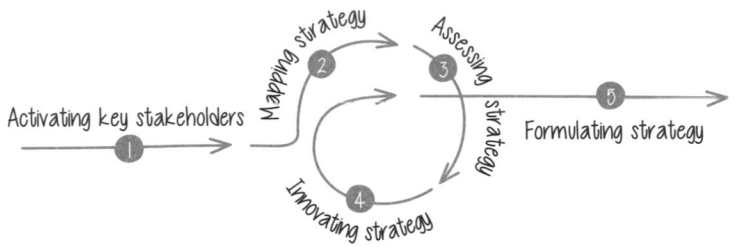

The five steps of strategy generation

Activating key stakeholders ①
② Mapping strategy
③ Assessing strategy
④ Innovating strategy
⑤ Formulating strategy

# The right mindset: How strategy experts think

With the content of this chapter so far you are well prepared to start the strategy generation process that you will find in the rest of the book. There is one more thing that I'd like to add, though. Next to all the ideas, tools, and examples that you will find in the remainder of the book, it helps quite a lot if you start with the right mindset. And where can we find this better than in what some of the most iconic CEOs and entrepreneurs say about their approach to strategy? After all, they have been quite successful. Therefore, I have gathered some inspirational quotes from Steve Jobs, Richard Branson, Larry Page, and Howard Schultz that show their mindset in doing business.

## Steve Jobs (co-founder and former CEO of Apple)

Probably the most quoted businessman and a great source of inspiration for many people, Steve Jobs became infamous for his way of running Apple. In relation to strategy generation, I find the following quotes particularly inspiring because of the strong emphasis they put on trusting your intuition and creativity.

> *"You can't connect the dots looking forward; you can only connect them looking backwards. So you have to trust that the dots will somehow connect in your future. You have to trust in something – your gut, destiny, life, karma, whatever. This approach has never let me down, and it has made all the difference in my life."*

*"Don't let the noise of other's opinions drown out your own inner voice. And most important, have the courage to follow your heart and intuition. They somehow already know what you truly want to become. Everything else is secondary."*

*"Creativity is just connecting things. When you ask creative people how they did something, they feel a little guilty because they didn't really do it, they just saw something. It seemed obvious to them after a while. That's because they were able to connect experiences they've had and synthesize new things."*

## Richard Branson (founder and CEO of Virgin Group)

Another iconic businessman and entrepreneur, Richard Branson is a well-known role model for many ambitious entrepreneurs. Like Steve Jobs, he emphasizes the importance of trusting in yourself and your ideas. As the following quotes illustrate, he is also a strong proponent of a learning-by-doing approach to strategy generation and business more generally.

*"You don't learn to walk by following rules. You learn by doing, and by falling over."*

*"Do not be embarrassed by your failures, learn from them and start again."*

*"A business has to be involving, it has to be fun, and it has to exercise your creative instincts."*

*"I never get the accountants in before I start up a business. It's done on gut feeling, especially if I can see that they are taking the mickey out of the consumer."*

*"To me, business isn't about wearing suits or pleasing stockholders. It's about being true to yourself, your ideas and focusing on the essentials."*

## Larry Page (co-founder and CEO of Google)

Both fervently celebrated and criticized, Google is amongst the most successful and influential companies today. Less visible than Steve Jobs and Richard Branson, its CEO Larry Page, has also said interesting things. I particularly like his emphasis on change and the idea that it can be done collaboratively with limited resources.

> *"Many leaders of big organizations, I think, don't believe that change is possible. But if you look at history, things do change, and if your business is static, you're likely to have issues."*

> *"If you can run the company a bit more collaboratively, you get a better result, because you have more bandwidth and checking and balancing going on."*

> *"You don't need to have a 100-person company to develop that idea."*

## Howard Schultz (CEO of Starbucks)

Probably the least well-known CEO in this group of four, Howard Schultz is another great source of inspiration if we look at his views on strategy and business. What I particularly like about the following quotes is his emphasis on dreams and ambitions, and on taking responsibility for realizing them.

> *"In life, you can blame a lot of people and you can wallow in self-pity, or you can pick yourself up and say, 'Listen, I have to be responsible for myself.'"*

> *"I believe life is a series of near misses. A lot of what we ascribe to luck is not luck at all. It's seizing the day and accepting responsibility for your future. It's seeing what other people don't see. And pursuing that vision."*

> *"Any business today that embraces the status quo as an operating principle is going to be on a death march."*

> *"This may sound a bit naive, but I got here by believing in big dreams."*

> *"I despise research. I think it's a crutch."*

> *"Great opportunities can be and have been created during tough economic times."*

Are these quotes representative of how successful organizations are run? Probably not. I have been selective about the people I quote and what quotes I've included here to make my point. But my goal was not to give an objective summary of what the average CEO thinks about strategy. No, my goal is to show the mindset of some of the most iconic CEOs so that we can learn from them. I hope these examples inspire you to start the strategy generation process with a similar mindset. If they have built their companies based on intuition, creativity, collaboration, learning, and taking responsibility, why wouldn't the same work for you?

# Introducing the
## four examples

Throughout the following chapters I turn to four example organizations to illustrate all the elements and steps of strategy generation. In order to anonymize them, all four are based on a mix of real organizations plus a bit of fantasy. Thus, although based on real organizations, the examples are strictly fictional. Together, they cover a broad variety of organizations: Large and small, young and old, product-based and service-based, and for-profit and non-profit. In this way, there should always be one or two that you can relate to.

I've chosen four fairly 'normal' organizations as examples. It might well be inspirational to use exceptional examples such as Apple, Virgin, Google, or Starbucks, and we can learn from the mindsets of their CEOs. However, 'normal' examples that are closer to the everyday practice of most organizations are easier to translate into your own situation and as such are more helpful. Therefore, the following four organizations will be our companions for the rest of the book:

## Macman – the solid machine manufacturer

**Size:** 223 people          **Turnover:** € 26 million          **Age:** 52 years

| | |
|---|---|
| **Main product:** | Steel processing machines (2 large customers) |
| **Led by:** | Director Ivo and a management team of 4 |
| **Strategic challenge:** | What could be our next big idea? Macman has done well with its current line of steel bending and cutting machines. The market is shrinking though, and the company needs an alternative core product to rely on. |

## Hospicare – the businesslike general hospital

**Size:** 4412 people          **Turnover:** € 358 million          **Age:** 31 years

**Led by:** A 4-person board of directors with Ingrid as chairman

**Main product:** General healthcare (1109 beds)

**Strategic challenge:** How to compete in a changing market? Hospicare has long provided general healthcare, just like other general hospitals. Changes in regulations and increasing competition though, ask for specialization and choices.

## GoforIT – the fast growing IT new venture

**Size:** 21 people          **Turnover:** € 2.3 million          **Age:** 4 years

**Led by:** Frank (commercial) and Liu (technology)

**Main product:** Online financial software and apps

**Strategic challenge:** How to grow in a sustainable manner? GoforIT has so far mainly relied on enthusiasm and creativity. Things are going very well now but to grow further they need more structure in everything they do.

## Comcom – the freelance communication advisor

**Size:** 1 person          **Turnover:** € 50 thousand          **Age:** 13 years

**Led by:** Anisha

**Main product:** Communication plans, PR, and text writing

**Strategic challenge:** How to grow and at the same time enjoy work more? Anisha wants to remain on her own and faces two strategic challenges: How to distinguish herself from others and how to increase revenue and impact without simply working more.

# Activating key stakeholders

This chapter presents the first step of the strategy generation process: Activating key stakeholders. It explains what this step entails and why it is needed. It also presents five activation tactics that you can use to successfully perform it.

> *Activating key stakeholders:*
> **Making key persons in the organization receptive to new strategy and mobilizing the resources needed for strategy generation.**

## The activation challenge

The first step of the strategy generation process is activating key stakeholders in the organization. Key stakeholders are those persons in the organization that have a big say in whether a new strategy will be adopted or not, and whether the organization will engage in strategy generation in the first place. You can think of the owners, the CEO, the (rest of the) board, the management team, or anyone else who makes key decisions for the organization or has an influential role throughout the strategy generation process. At this step you try to convince these people to remain open-minded and motivated during a process of new strategy generation. As such, this step helps you make them receptive to new strategy and mobilize the resources needed for strategy generation.

In most organizations this step is necessary initially because the development of new strategy happens far from automatically. There is often a tendency not to pay sufficient attention to strategy generation, or to start too late. If in your organization the key stakeholders are already convinced (or if you're just on your own), you could probably skip this step. In all other cases though, it is essential as a start of the strategy generation process.

What you are trying to do at this step is to turn an organization that is strategically inactive and primarily concerned with strategy execution into one that is strategically active and also engaged in strategy generation. In other words, it helps break out of the strategy execution cycle into a strategy generation cycle.

## The activation challenge: Breaking out of the strategy execution cycle

Strategy generation cycle

Strategy execution cycle

The strategy execution cycle is characterized by a focus on the short term and by being primarily concerned with running the organization and performing its day-to-day activities. It also includes efforts to make these activities more efficient (or 'lean'), faultless (through quality management initiatives and continuous improvement), and cheaper (by cost-cutting, automation, standardization and so forth). All these activities are important for an organization since they enable it to perform and improve its primary activities.

> "Make sure the organization starts thinking about new strategy on time and with sufficient drive and ambition."

However, there is a limit to what can be done in terms of efficiency, quality, and costs. At some point in time further improvement along this line can only be marginal or close to zero. It is often at that point that organizations start realizing they need to try something new and change their strategy. And often this is too late since there is no time or money left and there are no suitable people anymore to engage in a strategy generation process. Activation is needed to avoid these situations and to make sure that the organization starts thinking about new strategy on time and with sufficient drive and ambition.

# Excuses and causes for strategic inactivity

To understand how you can activate your organization so that it starts engaging in strategy generation, it is useful to first get a sense of the reasons why organizations are strategically inactive. We can divide them into common but invalid excuses, and genuine but avoidable causes.

## Common (but invalid) excuses for strategy inactivity

It is quite easy to find excuses to avoid engaging in strategy generation. Over the past years I've heard quite a number of them from CEOs, managers, and entrepreneurs that show how they resist. The following ten are my favorites:

1 **No time. Too busy with running the business.**
Invalid because this simply means setting the wrong priorities. Of course it is attractive to focus on the short term only, but if there's anything that research shows, it is that organizations that also give priority to strategic innovation perform better.

2 **No money. We have a crisis and must cut costs first.**
Invalid for the same reason. It just shows that the organization has set the wrong priorities in the past and is stuck in strategy execution now. Usually, the crisis itself is a result of this and, although attractive, it cannot be attributed to external forces. Of course times may be difficult, but at the end only the organization itself can do something about it, so blaming others is of no use.

3 **No use. We're at the mercy of what happens around us.**
Invalid because it victimizes the organization too much and underestimates its power and autonomy. Of course you depend on your environment. But you can influence it as well, even in

highly regulated industries such as health care. You always have some freedom in choosing your environment and in doing things differently from others.

4   Not allowed. Headquarters or my boss doesn't allow us.
Invalid because this victimizes the person saying it too much. Of course, some organizations provide little room for creativity and strategic thinking through strict rules and regulations. However, usually this excuse exaggerates the strictness of the rules and regulations. We can assume that they were set for the benefit of the organization. But if breaking them helps more, there is a good chance you will get more room. So, why not show some civil – or organizational – disobedience and bend the rules in a way that you think is beneficial for the organization?

5   No need. We are doing fine without strategy.
Invalid because it isn't true. Every organization has a strategy. Whether you are aware of it, though, is another question. The organization's strategy might not have been written down, but if you look at what the organization does today and what kind of decisions were made in the past, you can extract what its factual strategy is. This is why the next step (mapping strategy) is so important, as it gives you insight into the current, actual strategy of the organization.

6   Too small. Strategy is for big firms, not for us.
Invalid because it is nonsense. Strategy is for every organization, including one-person businesses. It is true that most strategy models and theories have been developed with large firms in mind. This, though, does not mean strategy is not relevant for small organizations. It doesn't even mean these models are not applicable; the large majority is.

7   Not applicable. We are a non-profit organization.
Invalid for a similar reason. The mere fact as to whether an organization is profit-oriented or not doesn't say anything about the relevance of strategy. In order to be successful, non-profits must also earn money and think about all ten elements of the Strategy Sketch. Only if there is no competition at all and customers are forced to buy your products and services is your organization in a position where strategy is not relevant. These cases are quite rare though.

8 Done that. We tried it, but it didn't work.

Invalid because it says more about the strategy generation capabilities of the organization than about the importance or applicability of strategy generation. It also signals a lack of perseverance. Okay, things might not have worked out well the first time, but failure is unavoidable, and rather than giving up it should be taken as a learning experience.

9 Too abstract. Strategy is too much blah blah.

Invalid because it only says something about how strategy is perceived, not about what strategy is actually about. I really understand this excuse, for strategy is often made bigger than it is and many strategy tools and approaches are rather abstract. However, this should not distract you from the fact that strategy is essential. I hope to show in this book that it can be very practical and concrete too.

10 No benefit. We don't need extensive plans.

Invalid because this only concerns a particular way of dealing with strategy, not strategy in general. I certainly agree that extensive plans are mostly not very useful, but this doesn't mean strategy itself is not useful. It just means that we need to find an effective way of strategy generation that doesn't rely on extensive plans.

Most of these excuses are either reasons not to engage in bad strategy generation or faulty reasons at all. As I hope to have shown though, they are not reasons not to engage in good strategy generation.

## "Both the excuses for strategic inactivity and its causes can be overcome."

### Genuine (but avoidable) causes of strategic inactivity

That we find so many excuses for not engaging in strategy generation is not so surprising. There are strong forces at play that are in favor of keeping things as they are. Generally, people and organizations have a tendency to go 'back to normal' and stay there as long as possible. Like an object that you throw in one direction, people and organizations tend to stay on the course they are on as long as there are no active impulses to change that course. In strategy there

43

are many organizational and psychological factors that cause this tendency. Key organizational ones include:

- **Path dependence.** Past strategies have led to the organization's current processes, technology, culture, and so forth. These cannot be easily changed.
- **Success trap.** Once things go well, there seems no reason to change it. Success even fosters investing more in what the organization already does.
- **Performance delay.** Today's performance is a result of yesterday's strategy. Signals that things may go worse come with a delay.

While these organizational causes of strategic inactivity may be quite strong, they can be overcome with a reasonable dose of common sense. Just being aware of them might already be sufficient because you can then take them into account. Psychological causes of inactivity, though, are harder to deal with, as they relate directly to the way people think. Rationally, the odds are quite obvious: Strategy generation is key to every organization's long-term health. So, if we were all rational, organizations would do much more about strategy generation and this step would not be necessary. However, as decades of research in cognitive psychology shows, we have all kind of non-rational biases that influence our decisions – and that means strategy generation often does not get the attention it deserves. Some of the important psychological causes of inactivity are:

- **Uncertainty avoidance.** People generally have a fear of the unknown. Since new strategy causes uncertainty, people naturally prefer to keep things as they are.
- **Confirmation bias.** People generally see what they like to see. Therefore they might be overoptimistic about the success and potential of the organization's current strategy.
- **Personal loss.** People have obtained particular positions that they like to keep. New strategy might harm those positions. Therefore, people may resist if they lose more than they gain.
- **Hubris and losing face.** Admitting that new strategy is needed may feel like admitting you were wrong - especially if you're late in initiating new strategy.
- **Conformation.** People generally like to do what others do – within the organization or in the industry. If this is the way things are apparently done, why change?

- **Escalation of commitment.** People like to be consistent. Once on a particular track, they are inclined to keep on investing in it – despite evidence that change is better.

Together, these organizational and psychological causes of inactivity make strategy generation a rather unlikely phenomenon to happen automatically in the average organization. But the good news is that there are several things you can do to overcome this. On the following pages you find five activation tactics that you can use for this.

| Activation tactic | What it does |
|---|---|
| 1. Open people's minds | Making new strategy *imaginable* |
| 2. Reveal the urgency | Making new strategy *unavoidable* |
| 3. Sell the benefits | Making new strategy *advantageous* |
| 4. Take away risks | Making new strategy *feasible* |
| 5. Just start | Making new strategy *happen* |

# Activation tactic 1:
# Open people's minds

The first activation tactic is making strategy *imaginable* by opening people's minds. The aim of this tactic is to take away the main barriers of imagination by challenging people's taken-for-granted ideas and assumptions. What you are trying to do with this tactic is to create awareness that things could be different from what they are. This is especially relevant if people have worked for a long time in one industry, for one organization, or in one function. There are several ways to do this.

## A Ask why the organization does what it does

You want to show people that it is not self-evident or even logical that the organization does what it does. One way is looking back at the past and ask *why* things are done the way they are done. Quite often, there are no rational reasons why a particular strategy is followed

## "Take away the main barriers of imagination by challenging people's taken-for-granted ideas and assumptions."

or why the organization is organized as it is. Instead, this may be a result of certain people working for the organization that left long ago (such as a previous director), or of certain technologies that were used. If you can make people realize that things are largely a result of circumstantial factors, this may help them to realize that things could easily have been different.

### B Show what has changed around you

Another useful tactic to open people's minds is to have them look at changes in the industry or in the broader society. Just look back ten years (or five) and look, for example, how new technologies (especially IT and mobile) have influenced the kind of products and services offered and the way of doing business today. You can show them these changes, but it is more powerful if they reveal the changes themselves. A simple exercise can be to ask them the five most important changes in the industry over the past ten years and have them rate the likelihood that similar kinds of changes will happen in the next ten years.

### C Let them draft a new organization

Often people find it very hard to look beyond the current organization. When you try to get them involved in strategy generation, they might tell you that nothing is possible, because the organization (structure, culture, size, ...) simply is at it is. One way to trigger their imagination is asking them what the organization and strategy should look like if they could start completely from scratch with a new organization (including a new legal entity) next to the existing one. Once they start thinking about that, there is a good chance that they will become enthusiastic and start realizing that what they are sketching could also work with the current organization – or that it is actually possible to start a completely new legal entity.

## $D$ Give examples of organizations that have changed radically

A fourth way to make new strategy imaginable is giving examples of organizations or industries that have gone through rather dramatic changes. The most powerful examples are those that the people in your organization can easily relate to. Therefore, it is preferable that you seek examples of organizations within your own industry, or of industries close to your own. If you can't come up with these examples, you can also use examples of well-known organizations that redefined their strategies. Some inspirational ones are:

1. **Nokia:** From paper mill to phone manufacturer.
2. **LEGO:** From relying on a patent to relying on user interaction.
3. **Xerox:** From photographic paper to copiers and printers.
4. **Philips:** From consumer electronics to health care.
5. **3M:** From mining and sand paper to tape and post-it notes.
6. **McDonalds:** From fast and fat to fast and healthy(ier)

If you don't know these examples well enough, just search them on the Internet. Wikipedia in particular is quite useful for this as it often gives a detailed account of the history of organizations.

# Activation tactic 2: Reveal the urgency

A second tactic for activating strategy generation is showing that new strategy is *unavoidable*. This includes creating the well-known 'sense of urgency' that is emphasized in change management approaches. The core of this tactic is signaling the problems associated with giving too limited attention to strategy generation before they turn into real problems. The following five tactics can be used for this.

## $A$ Ask whether the organization will still exist in five years

A simple tactic to reveal the need for new strategy is asking your key stakeholders whether the organization will still exist in five years if it just continues doing what it does today. This makes them think about ongoing developments in the organization's surroundings and whether the current strategy is appropriate for that. If their answer is no, you probably have them on board. Otherwise, you can continue with the next tactic.

## B Reveal internal signs of a need for new strategy

Another way to show that strategy generation is needed is letting people face facts. You want to show them signs indicating that the organization's strategy is reaching its expiration date or signs that reveal a lack of attention to strategy. These are ten key internal signs:

1. Over 80 % of revenue comes from existing products.
2. There is a strong dependence on a few large customers.
3. No significant new customers were attracted over the past year.
4. No significant new products/services were sold over the past year.
5. There is an increasing focus on cost-reduction and efficiency.
6. Margins and prices are decreasing or too low.
7. There is a defensive attitude towards the current business.
8. No significant changes in staff happened over the past year.
9. There is no strategy process or systematic attention to strategy.
10. The economy or others are blamed for bad results.

If you recognize three or more of these signs in your organization, this signals strategy requires more attention.

## C Reveal external signs of a need for new strategy

Also in the organization's environment there are signs indicating a need for new strategy. Ten important ones that you can use to convince key stakeholders to engage in new strategy generation are:

1. The demand for the kind of products you offer is shrinking.
2. The number of jobs in the industry is decreasing.
3. An increasing standardization of products/services is taking place.
4. Price competition is increasing or is already fierce.
5. Old competitors exit, are taken over, or go bankrupt.
6. New competitors come and do things differently.
7. New technologies enter the industry.
8. Industry boundaries are increasingly blurred.
9. Predictions are unreliable due to growing uncertainty.
10. The media are questioning the industry's viability.

The larger the number of signs you recognize here, the more urgently a new strategy is needed.

# "Signal the problems associated with too limited attention to strategy generation before they turn into real problems."

## *D* Fill out a BCG matrix

Another effective way to show the need for new strategy is filling out a BCG matrix. This is a two-by-two matrix developed by the Boston Consulting Group in which you categorize your products and services along two dimensions: market share and growth rate of the market. Based on these two dimensions, you get the following four categories:

- **Question marks** (low market share, high growth): new products or services for which it is unclear whether they will fly or not.
- **Stars** (high share, high growth): still new, but already and increasingly successful products or services.
- **Cash cows** (high share, low growth): usually the products/services on which the organization relies most. Mature and stable.
- **Dogs** (low share, low growth). Products and services that are on their return. Markets are shrinking and becoming less attractive.

You don't need to do extensive research for this. Just divide your products and services into the four categories based on your best knowledge. If the first two categories are relatively empty compared to the latter two, this is a clear signal that the organization's strategy requires renewal.

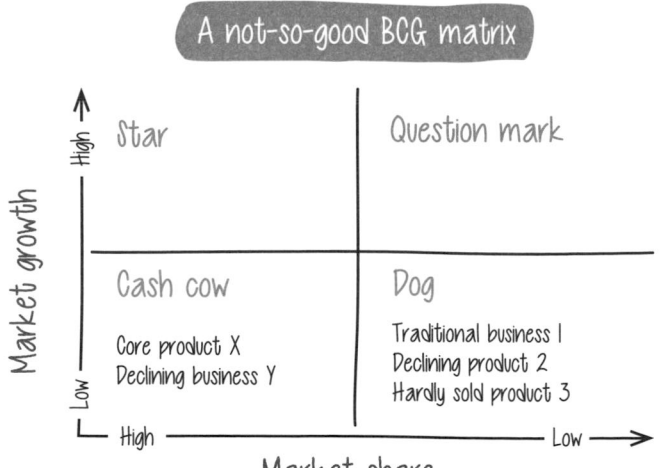

A not-so-good BCG matrix

|  | Star | Question mark |
| --- | --- | --- |
| **Cash cow** | **Dog** |

Star

Question mark

Cash cow
Core product X
Declining business Y

Dog
Traditional business 1
Declining product 2
Hardly sold product 3

Market growth — High / Low

Market share — High / Low

E Give examples

Examples work here too, especially of industries or companies that died or failed otherwise because of insufficient changes to their strategy. Like with the first activation tactic, examples close to your own organization are the most powerful. Otherwise, consider the following ones:

- **Record industry:** Redefined through digital music.
- **Newspaper and printing industry:** Having problems due to online content.
- **Kodak:** Failed to switch to digital photography.
- **Nokia:** No timely switch to smartphones.

Like with the examples mentioned earlier, you could just search the Internet for more information or consult Wikipedia. Also helpful are lists of declining industries or of jobs that will disappear in the not-so-distant future, mostly because of computerization. Search, for example, 'declining industries' or 'disappearing jobs' for inspiration or look for a study called 'The Future of Employment' conducted by the University of Oxford.

# Activation tactic 3: Sell the benefits

The next tactic to get the strategy generation process going is to show skeptics that new strategy is *advantageous* for the organization or for them personally. Whereas the previous tactic emphasized the perils of not engaging in strategy generation, this tactic emphasizes the possible gains of doing so.

A Emphasize organizational gains

The first thing you can do is to stress the organizational benefits of being engaged in new strategy generation. These include the following ten:

1. It motivates people and gives the organization new energy.
2. It avoids always focusing on costs and inefficiencies.
3. It leads to a more productive usage of the organization's potential.
4. It helps finding new or better sources of income.
5. It creates opportunities to make happier customers.
6. It helps to do things better and differently than your competitors.
7. It creates oversight and insight into the organization.
8. It fosters coherence and alignment of what the organization does.

⑨ It provides a good reason to get rid of unwanted things.
⑩ At some point you'll have to do it anyway, so why not now?

You probably have quite a good idea who will be sensitive to what arguments. So, instead of simply listing all these advantages it is better to emphasize those that will appeal most to your audience.

## B Emphasize personal gains

If showing organizational benefits is not enough, you can also stress the personal gains of new strategy generation. Obviously what these gains are precisely depends on the particular position and personality of your skeptic. So, here it would also be best if you know who is sensitive to what arguments. Generally, though, you can think of the following:

① It provides an opportunity to realize personal ideas or ambitions.
② It offers a possibility for getting rid of things they don't like.
③ It gives them influence on the organization's direction.
④ It helps safeguard or improve their position in the organization.
⑤ It provides an opportunity for showing what they are capable of.
⑥ It encourages learning new skills and gathering new experiences.
⑦ It gives a sense of pride if they are successful.
⑧ It makes it more likely that they can hire people rather than fire them.
⑨ It is fun - certainly more fun than cost cutting.
⑩ At some point they'll have to do it anyway, so why not now?

# "Show skeptics that new strategy is advantageous for the organization and for them personally."

## C Ask for people's dreams and ambitions

You could also turn it around. Rather than selling the organizational and individual benefits above, you can also ask people what they would like to achieve. They might have ideas, dreams or ambitions that they would like to realize for the organization or personally. These may be hidden, because people have already concluded it would be impossible to realize them and have given up. However, if you insist and ask what they would really like to achieve if everything were possible and if they had all the resources they needed, I bet

51

you would get some interesting answers. Then, your next question to them is when would it be more likely that they can realize their ambitions. Is this when the organization continues as it does, or when it starts working on a new strategy? Assuming their answer is the latter, you have sold them the benefits of engaging in new strategy generation.

## ⅅ Give examples

For this third tactic giving examples also works well. It also works best here if these are examples that people can easily relate to. For illustrating the organizational gains of strategy generation you should ideally use examples of organizations that are similar to yours and that have successfully changed their strategy. For illustrating the personal gains it helps to give examples of people that have personally gained from new strategy and that hold similar positions than the ones you are trying to convince. For both types of examples you can think of:

- A good competitor that has renewed its strategy.
- A customer or supplier which has reinvented itself.
- A similar-sized organization in another industry.
- An old organization that was unlikely to change but did.

If you can't find any good examples, you could also think of the usual suspects: Organizations and people that have been very successful as a result of constant improvement and innovation of their strategies and that are often used as examples. This includes Apple, Virgin, Google, Starbucks, and their leaders (see the quotes at the end of Chapter 2), or any other organization that has followed a successful strategy – Ikea, Coca Cola, Ryanair, 3M, Samsung, BMW, and so on.

# Activation tactic 4: Take away risks

A fourth activation tactic is making new strategy *feasible* for the organization and for your key stakeholders. After the previous tactics everyone might be convinced that new strategy needs to be generated. However, if major hurdles are seen, it still doesn't happen. The purpose of this fourth tactic is to take these hurdles away by reducing the risk of failure.

## A Limit organizational risks

For limiting the organizational risks associated with new strategy generation we can draw from a variety of tactics used in entrepreneurship. Since there will always be some failure, the core idea is to do it quickly and cheaply. To achieve this you could do one or more of the following:

- Invest time, resources, and money based on what you can afford to lose without harming the organization. In this way you decide upfront what your maximum investment will be and thereby control your risks.
- Isolate the actions and resources that are needed for the new strategy from the rest of the organization. This makes sure that the strategy generation process doesn't disturb the ongoing business.
- Install a step-by-step strategy process that requires a go/no-go decision before each step. This ensures that you can stop the process at any time before big investments are made.
- Postpone the 'point of no return' as far as possible. First focus on everything that can still be undone. This keeps you flexible and makes that you avoid agreeing on commitments that you later regret.
- When going live, start with a real-life pilot with customers that tells you whether the strategy works in practice. This makes sure that, if you fail, you fail cheaply and quickly.
- Share risks with customers, partners, or suppliers by involving them early on in the process. Make their success dependent on your success. This creates commitment and aligns interests.
- Sell before you actually make something. Try getting commitments before you make significant investments. This makes you depend less on sales estimates since you are already certain of some sales.

## "Since there will always be some failure, the core idea is to do it quickly and cheaply."

## B Limit personal risks

To convince people to engage in strategy generation, you also want to limit their personal risks. They might have a lot to lose from a new strategy – or at least they may think so. The following tactics help to limit this:

- Do all of the above to limit organizational risks. If the organizational risks are lower, people's personal risks are reduced as well, especially since your key stakeholders are usually the ones that are held accountable.
- Ask about their concerns and how these concerns could be taken away. Thus, instead of doing it yourself, let them provide the solutions. This tactic works well in sales, and it works equally well in strategy.
- Take responsibility. Make sure that you are to blame and not them if the new strategy fails. Of course this implies some risk on your side, but if you are convinced of the need for new strategy, why not take it?
- Share responsibility. Make sure that everyone is to blame if the new strategy fails. If strategy generation is a collaborative process in which many people are involved, the risks are shared as well.

## C  Get the affordable loss on the table

An important reason why organizations are not sufficiently strategically active is that people fear losing time, money, or face due to an unsuccessful new strategy. Arguing against this or trying to reassure them doesn't really work because why would you know better than them? You probably don't. And even if you know better, this still doesn't take away their uncertainty. What does work, though, is helping them specify their affordable loss – this is what people are willing to lose if things don't work out. Setting their affordable loss gives them control over the worst thing that could happen, and by giving control you reduce the uncertainty. So, what you want to do is ask people what time, money, or other resources they would be willing to invest in the generation of new strategy even if here is a substantial chance that they would lose it. This provides you with some sort of budget that can be used for strategy generation.

When you try to arrange this, you might need to help people a bit. They might think too easily just about money while forgetting other valuable resources that they are sitting on and actually would be willing to spend. Therefore to get as much as you can, it is handy to keep the checklist below with you, or in the back of your mind.

## Checklist of resources that people could invest in strategy generation

| Time & power-related resources such as: | Financial & material resources such as: | Intellectual & social resources such as: |
|---|---|---|
| Time | Money | Information |
| People | Machine-hours | Advice |
| Man-hours | Space | Judgments |
| Freedom | Materials | Ideas |
| Authority | Capacity | Contacts |
| Support | Tools | Energy |

## D Give examples

Examples work here too, particularly if people can relate to them. In this case you want to give examples of unlikely successes or of organizations or people that started with little and managed to grow it into a successful strategy without running major risks. If you don't have examples that are close to your organization, you can consider using the following ones:

- **eBay.** Pierre Omidyar started eBay in 1995 as a hobby project next to his fulltime job. He argues that precisely because time and money were limited, eBay has become so successful because it led to a simple product and organization without unnecessary features and staff.
- **Amazon.** Jeff Bezos started Amazon in 1994 with an investment by his parents and – how clichéd – in his own garage. Although he told his parents that there would be a 70% chance they would lose their money, they invested anyway.
- **Chipotle Mexican Grill.** Steve Ells started Chipotle in 1993 with the idea that it would be a cash cow from which he could later start a more fancy restaurant. It started very low profile with just burritos and tacos, and was put together very simply with plywood. The relatively small amount of money needed came from Ells's dad.

## "Do something that clearly deviates from the current strategy or that exemplifies the new strategic direction."

## Activation tactic 5: Just start

A last activation tactic is to simply start making new strategy *happen*. Instead of trying to convince people and waiting until they get moving, you can also be entrepreneurial and just start. Sometimes this is the best and easiest way to get the strategy generation process going. In this way you basically first skip the whole strategy generation process and immediately jump to execution – on a small scale. Once people see that your actions work out, you've set an example that might convince them to engage in strategy generation.

You want to do something that clearly deviates from the current strategy or that exemplifies the new strategic direction that you have in mind. It is also quite powerful if you can do something that your key stakeholders consider infeasible or too risky. If you cannot come up with something yourself, you might want to consider doing some of the following:

- **Get a quick win.** There might be low-hanging fruit that reflects the strategic direction you are anticipating, that is easy to realize, and that immediately has a positive impact. By taking these actions, you show that change is possible and that there are benefits to the new strategy
- **Get a new customer.** If the new strategy implies entering or creating a new market it may be fairly convincing if you can tell people you already have a first (potential) customer.
- **Find a new source of income.** One way to renew your strategy is to innovate the revenue model by finding new sources of income. So, what you can do is just trying to arrange this on a small scale. If, for example, your current revenue model is based on hourly rates for a service, you could just try and sell the same service for a fixed price. If this works, you have some evidence that change is possible.

- **Break a rule.** There might be some rules, habits, or structures in the organization that impede progress and cause new strategy not to get off the ground. To break out of this stalemate, you can do something that intentionally deviates from the norm. You can, for example, start working from home one day a week if that is uncommon and if it might support the new strategy that you have in mind.
- **Find an ally.** Instead of trying to convince key decision-makers you can also try to find someone in the organization that sympathizes with your ideas and who is also ready to act. By acting together, you can make more impact. And if he or she does the same, your impact might gradually spread throughout the organization.
- **Fail quickly and cheaply.** If the organization is risk-avoiding or if there is some fear of failure, you might want to deliberately fail. If you do this in such a way that the consequences are minor, this can show others in the organization that failure isn't as bad as they thought. This can be a bit risky, though, since your failure might also make people even less willing to engage in strategy generation.

# The four examples

## Strategy activation at Macman

It was evident to director Ivo and his management team that new strategy was unavoidable and advantageous. They were well aware change was needed. The main bottlenecks to actually starting were that they didn't really see how and just saw problems ahead. This meant their strategy needed to be made imaginable and feasible.

- **Making new strategy imaginable.** Macman's leadership was stuck in the mindset of "we are a machine manufacturer." What helped was looking back at their history – they were a producer of semi-finished steel products before they actually started making their own machines. Realizing this opened up their minds a bit. What worked even better was asking them numerous times "why?" and "why not?" until they realized that their minds were mainly shaped by assumptions than by unbreakable truths.
- **Making new strategy feasible.** They assumed new strategy meant hiring expensive consultants, spending a lot of time on analyzing, and writing extensive plans. They blew up strategy generation into something big. What helped was showing them that you can start small and work iteratively, relying in first instance mostly on the resources and competences the firm already had.

## Strategy activation at Hospicare

At Hospicare the main bottlenecks were convincing the board of directors that new strategy was unavoidable and advantageous. Although chairman Ingrid – through her previous jobs in business – was convinced they needed to look beyond the 'normal' health care business, the other members were more traditional and optimistic about the current strategy. They argued that "things have gone well, go well, and will keep on going well the way we do it."

Given the hospital's fact-based mentality, Ingrid figured she needed to give them 'hard' evidence that change was needed. So she asked her staff department to compile a report with a) the performance of the hospital over the past 10 years in terms of margins, innovation, and revenue, and b) an overview of developments in the hospital's environment in terms of competitors and demand for care. This worked. As it turned out, things hadn't gone so well and weren't going well at all. This convinced the rest of the board that things certainly would not go well if they didn't change their strategy. Furthermore, Ingrid managed to show the personal benefits of strategic change. The board members were all quite proud and sensitive about their positions and achievements. She used this by reminding them how a successful change would be good for their careers.

## Strategy activation at GoforIT

At GoforIT strategy activation was not needed. They clearly didn't lack imagination and saw plenty of opportunities to grow, expand, or even redefine the company. Also, feasibility was not an issue since they were convinced of their own abilities. They were also aware that they needed to do something given their fast growth over the past 3 years. There were increasing internal problems and a lack of structure and focus in their activities. So it was evident that actually having a strategy was unavoidable and advantageous.

## Strategy activation at Comcom

For Anisha it was quite clear that she should change her strategy. Change was not so much unavoidable – she could go on like before for many years without any real problems – but she really wanted it because she saw a lot of advantages (more fun, more money, more time). Like Macman, her main bottlenecks were related to the imaginability and feasibility of new strategy. She had secretly imagined how to redefine her business (she dreamt of becoming a famous food blog writer), but could not see how she could do that. What worked well in her case was looking at inspirational examples of some well-known blog writers and journalists and just telling her to start now alongside her current job. The risks and costs of this were minor and if it didn't work out she could still rely on her current business.

# 4 Mapping strategy

This fourth chapter presents Step 2 of the strategy generation process: Mapping strategy. It explains how the Strategy Sketch can be used to map an organization's strategy along with its ten core elements. It also provides various questions, exercises, checklists, useful models, and examples for doing this. Because I need to discuss all ten elements, the chapter is a bit lengthy. Yet, you can of course just pick those elements you want to read or use.

> *Mapping strategy*
> **Identifying the organization's strategy by describing it on the basis of its ten core elements.**

## The meaning and role of mapping strategy

As a second step of the strategy generation process, mapping strategy is about identifying the organization's strategy by describing it on the basis of the ten elements of the Strategy Sketch. At this step you make the organization's strategy explicit. As noted earlier, I don't mean the organization's formal strategy. If there is one, it is usually written down and relatively easy to identify. What I mean, though, is the organization's actual strategy as is reflected in what the organization does. This step plays at least four important roles in the strategy generation process:

A **Understanding.** By making all ten elements of the strategy explicit, this step reveals what is underneath the strategy as it is formulated. As such, this step creates an in-depth understanding of the organization's current strategy.

B **Communication.** Mapping the organization's strategy also provides a means to talk about strategy in a coherent manner.

61

# Step 2

With the Strategy Sketch as a basis, this step makes sure that everybody talks about the same thing when they use the word 'strategy.'

C **Revealing ambiguity.** Mapping also helps find blind spots and ambiguities in the organization's strategy. While you are mapping all ten elements you may find out that you need more information about some, or that there is substantial disagreement.

D **Stepping-stone.** As part of the strategy generation process, mapping strategy is also a stepping-stone to the next steps. The mere act of mapping out your strategy might already reveal some points for improvement and directions for new strategy. In some cases you might not even have to move on to the next steps.

## How to use the tools

Chapter 2 introduced you to the Strategy Sketch and its core elements. Based on that chapter you have a sense of what the ten elements mean and why they are important for strategy. In this chapter you find further information and tools that help you actually map out your strategy along these ten elements. For each element, you find the following tools:

- **Questions to ask.** Two sets of questions that help you a) assess what the element currently looks like in your organization, and b) come up with new directions.
- **Beyond-the-obvious exercises.** Simple exercises that help you look beyond what first comes to the mind. With these exercises you can ensure that the mapping of your strategy has sufficient depth.
- **Inspirational checklists.** A list of ideas that can help you check whether you considered enough options for a particular element or maybe some you have overseen. These also help you to think about new directions.
- **Useful models.** Some useful models that help deepen your understanding of the element. No full explanations are given, but you can easily search them on the Internet or use pages such as www.mindtools.com or www.12manage.com or Wikipedia to learn more about them.

While going through the following pages it can be useful to immediately start mapping your strategy. For this it is handy if you draw the Strategy Sketch (see page 24) on an empty DIN A3 / Tabloid format paper, or download and print it off from www.thestrategyhandbook.com. While reading about each element below, you can then already start filling in your Strategy Sketch with the first ideas that come to mind.

> Tip:
> Print or draw an empty Strategy Sketch and start filling it in while you read further.

# 1 Resources & competences

Although you could start by mapping any element of the Strategy Sketch, I personally prefer to start with your resources and competences. This makes you first look at the organization itself and understand what you have, what you are good at, and what makes you unique. In this way you start close to home with what you already have at your disposal. When you start mapping this, it is useful to take the following into account:

- Don't make long or complete lists of resources and competences. Focus on the most important ones; those that make you special.
- Your most valuable and unique resources or competences can be quite unexpected. They need not even be related to your core products or services. They can for instance be your selection and hiring process.
- Look at combinations of resources/competences. The reason you're good at something is usually a combination of factors. For example, it may be because of your particular knowledge, equipment, people *and* location that you outperform others.
- Dig deeper by asking 'why' a couple of times to find out which competences lie beneath a particular resource or competence.
- Be aware that expert entrepreneurs prefer adjusting their strategy to their available means rather than striving for hard-to-reach means. So why wouldn't you do the same?

# Step 2

## Questions to ask

| For assessing your *current* resources and competences: | For using or developing *new* resources and competences: |
| --- | --- |
| • Which means do you have that others don't? | • What else can you do with your resources and competences? |
| • What are you really good at that others can't do or find difficult? | • How can you make them more unique or valuable? |
| • What slack resources or unused capacity do you have access to? | • How can you protect them better against imitation? |
| • What would you miss most when it is gone? | • What means can you easily obtain, but others not or with difficulty? |
| • What competences allowed you to get or develop your current resources and competences? | • What resources or competences should you let go, outsource, or sell to others? |

## Beyond-the-obvious exercise

When asking someone about their most important resources and competences it is quite common to get responses such as "our people," "our knowledge," or "our culture." These general responses are not the most useful ones for strategy generation. To get more in-depth responses, you can do the following simple exercise. Let people imagine there has been a big fire or another disaster and that the whole organization has been destroyed. Then you ask them one of the following two questions: "What would be the thing that you miss most and that can only with difficulty be replaced or rebuilt?" or "What would be the minimum that you need to restart the organization and that you cannot buy elsewhere?" In this way you get the really essential and unique resources and competences on the table.

## Inspirational checklist

To identify your best resources and competences, consider whether compared to others you perhaps have the...

- ...most efficient way of working.
- ...cheapest or fastest way of producing or delivering.
- ...best location for suppliers or customers.
- ...best access to people or resources.
- ...most advanced or smartest technology.
- ...best skilled, creative, or intelligent people.
- ...friendliest and most loved staff or representatives.
- ...most loyal customers or employees.
- ...most effective selection, hiring, or development program.
- ...largest or best network of partners.
- ...largest or most complete facilities.
- ...biggest pockets or best financial situation.
- ...strongest or most trustworthy brand.
- ...best ability to involve customers or suppliers.
- ...best domain name or online findability.
- ...best design skills in terms of esthetics or usability.

## Useful models

**For assessing the quality of your resources and competences:** Barney's VRINE model, suggesting that resources should be:

- **A** **Valuable.** They should enable your value proposition so that they help to create value for customers.
- **B** **Rare.** They should be unique so that not every competitor has them too.
- **C** **Inimitable.** They should be difficult to imitate so that they remain valuable and unique even if your competitors try to do better.
- **D** **Non-substitutable.** They should be hard to substitute so that your competitors cannot simply find another way of doing the same.
- **E** **Exploitable.** It should be possible to effectively and efficiently use them by your organization; otherwise they remain useless.

**For understanding the few things that your organization is really good at and that form the basis for its success:** Hamel and Prahalad's Core competence approach. Freely based on their definition, a core competence is a combination of resources, knowledge, skills, and capabilities that enables your organization to perform one or more processes on a world-class level (or at

65

least very good). Also helpful is their metaphor of a tree to explain core competences:

- **End products:** The products or services that you sell to your customers. They are the leaves of the tree.
- **Core products:** The building blocks on which various end products are based. These can be, e.g., particular technologies or service modules. These are the trunk and branches of the tree.
- **Core competences:** The underlying competences that enable your organization to deliver the core products. These are the roots of the tree.

**For understanding how balancing specialization and integration is key to the success of organizations:** Grant's notion of knowledge integration. On the one hand organizations need specialized resources (you, for example, want your people to be excellent at something, not mediocre at everything), but on the other hand integration needs to take place as well (otherwise they will not work together or fail to combine their contributions). Integration can be achieved by various means including:

(A) Giving rules and directives, by telling people exactly what to do.
(B) Sequencing of tasks, such as at an assembly line.
(C) Creating organizational routines, by standardizing processes.
(D) Using autonomous teams and leave it up to people themselves to integrate.

Also important is a common language and shared understanding in the organization so that people can actually communicate and collaborate.

# 2 Partners

After identifying your resources and competences, a natural next step is to complete mapping your means by identifying your key partners. These are the people and organizations that you work with and that make your products or services more valuable. While identifying them take the following into account:

- Your network could be quite unique and hard to copy. If so, it could give you a competitive advantage next to resources and competences.

- Look carefully at what is your unique value compared to your partners' unique value. You might depend too much on their strengths rather than on your own. This makes you vulnerable and over-dependent.
- Take some time to look at all your personal offline and online contacts. Which of them could you use in your organization?
- Also think about unusual partnerships that you could make - this helps you to think outside the box and to come up with innovative strategies.
- Research shows that effective networks are a combination of a few strong relationships and a diverse set of weaker relationships. Check your network and use this to your advantage.
- Do as expert entrepreneurs do: Carefully select partners but also let them select you. Let the world know you are open to new partnerships and see what comes of it.

## Questions to ask

| For identifying your *current* partners: | For finding *new* partners or using them better: |
|---|---|
| • With which organizations are there formal contracts? | • What can your partners do more for you than they currently do? What unused means do they have? |
| • Who does the organization depend on or frequently work with? | |
| | • Who benefits from your organization or has similar interests but doesn't work with you yet? |
| • Which organizations support or help you most? | |
| • Who do you know? Who is in your own network or that of colleagues? | • What organizations would you find attractive to work with? And which ones would like to work with you? |
| • What useful contacts do your partners have? | • Which partners are not beneficial for you and you are better off without? |

# Step 2

## Beyond-the-obvious exercise

When you map your partners there is a risk that you just list the obvious organizations that you work closely with. A useful exercise giving a different view on who your (potential) partners are is drawing a customer-centered stakeholder map. A stakeholder map contains the people and organizations relevant to your organization. Rather than putting the organization itself at the center, though, you put the customer at the center. Around that you draw two circles. The inner circle contains those people and organizations that directly influence your customer; and the outer circle contains the ones with an indirect influence. Once you finish the picture, you should ask yourself how many of them you already work or collaborate with. The rest are your potential partners.

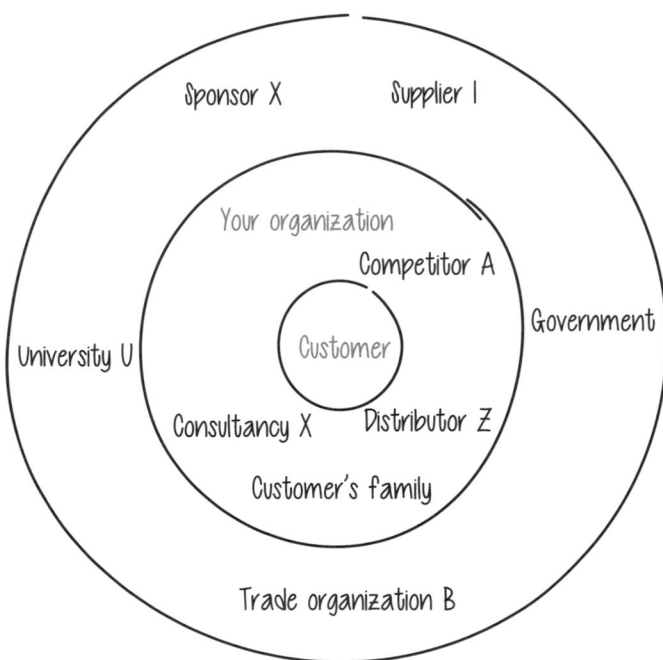

Example of a customer-centered stakeholder map

## Inspirational checklist

To identify your partners and the reasons they are important, consider whether these already include or could include particular...

- ...customers, for co-creating your products/services.
- ...suppliers, for innovating your products/services.
- ...competitors, for joining forces against others.
- ...universities, for gaining advanced knowledge.
- ...schools, for hiring well-educated employees.
- ...accountancy firms, for accessing new customers.
- ...local or regional governments, for obtaining funding.
- ...distributors, for getting your products to customers.
- ...interest groups, for working for the same purpose.
- ...trade or industry associations, for representing you.
- ...investors for obtaining funding, contacts, or advice.
- ...complementors (offering products that are complementary to yours) for better serving the market.
- ...local communities for creating goodwill.
- ...media for creating positive publicity.
- ...celebrities for increasing the desirability of products.
- ...artists or designers for thinking outside the box.

## Useful models

**For understanding the kind of relationships that you may have with others:** Granovetter's distinction between strong and weak ties.

- *Strong ties* are contacts who you know well and have a strong bond with. You cannot handle too many of these as they take time to maintain.
- To keep your network diverse, you should also have a larger network of *weak ties* – contacts that could be valuable for your organization, but that require less or no maintenance.

A good network contains a mix of both. This guarantees you have a network that is sufficiently diverse to keep you informed about a large variety of possibly relevant topics and that is sufficiently strong to make sure you also get something done through actual collaboration.

**For understanding your position in your network:** Burt's notions of 'structural holes' and 'small worlds'. The small world idea says that the world is subdivided into groups within which people are closely connected (small worlds), but between which there are no or only

69

few connections. You have a structural hole position if you are one of the few people that connects two or more of these small worlds. This position gives you important benefits since you can combine things others cannot. You could, for example, have good connections in two industries because of some previous jobs you had. This position might make you one of the few who could use the insights of one industry in the other. So, you should have a look at your own network and assess whether you are connecting two or more 'small worlds' and whether you could use this position to your benefit.

**For evaluating and selecting suitable partners:** Carter's Ten Cs of supplier evaluation. The following criteria can help select the right partners – not just suppliers, but any other type of partner too:

1. **Competency:** Does the partner have the competences you need and at the right level?
2. **Capacity:** Does the partner have sufficient capacity to work with you and to fulfill your requirements?
3. **Commitment:** Is the partner committed to delivering the required quality and to you as a partner?
4. **Control:** Is the partner in control of its processes?
5. **Cash:** Is the partner financially healthy?
6. **Cost:** Are your partner's prices attractive?
7. **Consistency:** Can the partner deliver the same quality of products or services consistently?
8. **Culture:** Do the partner's values and goals match yours and do you get along personally?
9. **Clean:** Is the partner sufficiently sustainable in terms of social and ecological impact?
10. **Communication:** Does the partner communicate well enough and in an appropriate manner?

# 3 Customers & needs

After mapping the means of the organization I usually move to the market side of the Strategy Sketch; to customers and needs and to competitors. So, the next element in line is customers and needs. This element concerns the people and organizations that you serve and which of their needs of you fulfill. The following things are useful to take into account for this element:

- See customers as people and understand their needs and concerns. In business-to-business, for example, know how purchasers are rewarded.
- Also take into account your customers' customers. Look at what their needs are and how this affects your customer.
- Decide whether you want to target a large and broad market or a specific niche. Usually the latter is easier and more realistic to start with.
- Make choices and avoid naïve reasoning such as "Our product is for everyone" or "There are 7 billion people, if only 0.001 % would…"
- Act as an expert entrepreneur: Postpone extensive market analysis, but estimate whether the total market is large enough and whether there is room for improvement. Then focus on actually getting customers.

## Questions to ask

| For understanding your *current* customers: | For finding *new* customers or serving customers better: |
|---|---|
| • What common characteristics do your customers have? | • Can you make your customers more loyal or buy more? |
| • What people use or pay for the product/service and who makes or influences the buying decisions? | • Do your customers have needs that you could also fulfill? |
| • What are these people's needs so that they can do what they need to do? | • Who could your customers recommend you to or who else is within reach of your network? |
| • Which of their problems can or do you solve? | • Who is currently not yet served but would benefit from your product? |
| • What are they willing to pay for? | • Which customers are you better off without? Who costs you more than you benefit? |

## Beyond-the-obvious exercise

An exercise borrowed from the business model guys: Make an empathy map. An empathy map is a sheet of paper divided into six blocks with six questions helping you to place yourself in the position of a customer (see the picture below). This helps you getting a more advanced understanding of their needs and concerns. The simplest way to do this exercise is to keep a specific customer in mind and answer the questions for that customer. You can repeat this for various customers. If you want to know more about this exercise, there is an entire book about it by Alexander Osterwalder et al., called 'Value proposition design.'

**Empathy map**

| What does s/he THINK? | What does s/he SEE and HEAR? | What are his/her PAINS? |
|---|---|---|
| What does s/he FEEL? | What does s/he SAY and DO? | What are his/her GAINS? |

## Inspirational checklist 1 (for identifying customers)

To identify potential customers, look at people or organizations that...

- ...walk away from your competitors.
- ...dislike your current product (but might like another variant).
- ...dislike generally what is offered by the industry.
- ...would never become customers now.
- ...are located in a very different country.
- ...have much more or less money to spend.
- ...are much younger or older than current customers.
- ...would use the product or service for something else.
- ...would use the product or service in a different way.
- ...don't yet know that they could benefit from the product.

- ...would be willing to accept a lower quality product or service.
- ...look for much higher quality.
- ...would appreciate features currently not offered.
- ...don't need the features currently offered.
- ...weren't there three years ago.
- ...are currently your competitors, suppliers, or partners.
- ...have changed quite radically over the past few years.

## Inspirational checklist 2 (for identifying customer needs)

To identify the needs of the persons or organizations that use or pay for your product/service, or who make or influence the buying decisions, consider for example whether they have the need to...

- ...save time or speed up.
- ...save money or get a reduction.
- ...reduce the risks that they bear.
- ...feel more secure.
- ...focus on what they like or are good at.
- ...get a particular job done.
- ...have fun or be entertained.
- ...boost or maintain their status.
- ...express their identity.
- ...connect with other people.
- ...improve their physical condition.
- ...improve their mental or emotional condition.
- ...enjoy convenience.
- ...try something new.
- ...improve themselves or achieve something.
- ...act in good conscience or ease their mind.

## Useful models

**For conducting systematic market research and choosing a promising market segment:** Kotler's classical three step 'STP' marketing process:

1. **Segmenting:** Divide the total market into parts based on a set of relevant criteria as age, income, size, personality, location, and so on.
2. **Targeting:** Choose the most promising segment based on an analysis of customer needs and competitors.
3. **Positioning:** Choose a value proposition that is different from those already on the market.

**For getting a sense of the different needs that people may have:** Maslow's Hierarchy of needs, proposing that people have 5 levels of needs:

1. **Physiological needs (lowest level):** Basic needs such as food, water, warmth, sex, or sleep.
2. **Safety needs:** Security and protection of family, health, property, resources, or employment.
3. **Love or belonging needs:** Friendship, love, intimacy, sense of belonging.
4. **Esteem needs:** Self-esteem, confidence, respect for and by others, prestige, achievement.
5. **Self-actualization needs (highest level):** Realizing one's full potential, using creativity, acceptance of facts, morality.

The idea of this hierarchy is that before you can move on to meeting a higher-level need you should first have fulfilled the levels below that.

**For recognizing what customers are most beneficial for you and for generating more loyal customers:** Christopher, Payne and Ballantyne's Ladder of loyalty, distinguishing six levels of loyalty:

1. **Suspect:** Might be interested but you don't know.
2. **Prospect:** Interested in your products/services.
3. **Customer:** Buys your products/services.
4. **Client:** Repeatedly buys your products/services.
5. **Supporter:** Actively recommends your products.
6. **Partner:** Actively works with the organization.

The higher up the ladder (down on this list), the more valuable the customer is for your organization.

# 4 Competitors

To complete the market side of the Strategy Sketch, the next element in line is competitors. Mapping them gives you a good understanding of who they are, how strong they are, and how you are different from them. When you do this, you should take the following into account:

- You need competitors, if only to compare yourself to when positioning yourself for your customers. Having good competitors can even be beneficial, as they help establish a healthy market.
- Think broadly about who your competitors might be. Substitutes can be broad and unexpected. Jewelry and expensive cars, for example, are very different products, but are substitutes for expressing identity.
- Also think about complementors: People or organizations that offer products/services that add value to yours (e.g. DVDs and DVD players).
- Although you should generally try to do things differently from your competitors, being too unique can also be dangerous. This is especially the case if your customer wants dual sourcing (at least one other organization that can offer the same products/services as you).
- Take into account that being a competitor is a role that people and organizations can take. At another point, they may also be partners.
- Connect to other elements. What makes you special, for example, in terms of value proposition, resources and competences, or partners?

## Questions to ask

For understanding *current and potential* competitors:

- What organizations offer similar products or services than you?

- Who could easily start offering something similar?

- Who offers products that substitute yours?

- With whom or what will customers compare you?

- Who makes your life most difficult and vice versa?

For finding ways to *avoid or benefit* from competitors:

- Can you use your competitors' strengths to your advantage?

- Who do you want your customers to compare you to?

- How could you make your competitors irrelevant?

- Where in or outside the industry is there less competition?

- What competitors are beneficial for you? Can you join forces?

# Step 2

## Beyond-the-obvious exercises

I assume you have quite a good sense of who your most important direct competitors are. But you also want to map those that are off your current radar. There are two short exercises that you can do to identify them. For the first exercise make a list of 5-7 keywords that describe your unique products or services and some of their unique features. Then start searching the Internet using these keywords. You'll be surprised about the organizations that show up. Given that they are found using 'your' keywords makes it quite likely that they are important competitors. Thus, this first exercise helps to identify competitors offering similar products to you. The second exercise helps you to think more in terms of substitutes. For this exercise ask two questions: "What if your company never "existed, how would customers satisfy their needs?" and "What if your industry never existed, what alternatives might satisfy your customers' needs?"

## Inspirational checklist

To identify ways in which you could be hindered less by competitors or even benefit from them, consider for example whether and how you can...

- ...collaborate, merge, or form an alliance with them.
- ...share information or other resources with them.
- ...license your technology to them so that you benefit from every product they sell.
- ...convince them or make it attractive for them to sell your products or services.
- ...serve customers that they cannot serve.
- ...learn from what they do wrong and do better.
- ...find out what they do and make sure you do what they don't.
- ...make them irrelevant by creating a new market.
- ...offer your products to a new type of customer.
- ...add or increase particular features of your products.
- ...reduce or omit particular features from your products.
- ...exploit your unique resources and competences and thus focus on what you can do better than them.
- ...do something that they would not expect from you.

## Useful models

**For making a comprehensive analysis of your competitors:** Porter's Five forces framework, which distinguishes five types of competitors:

1. **Industry competitors:** Your competitors in the narrow sense of the word.
2. **Suppliers:** You compete with your suppliers too, for example about price.
3. **Customers:** Same here; you compete with them in the same way as with your suppliers.
4. **Substitutes:** Organizations offering products or services that could substitute yours.
5. **New entrants:** Not actual but potential future competitors that could enter the industry.

The goal of this analysis is to assess the attractiveness of the industry by diagnosing the strength of all five.

**For differentiating (the value of) your products and services from those of competitors:** Kim and Mauborgne's Blue ocean 'Strategy canvas.' This is a visual diagram with two axes that help you to systematically compare the various offers that are present in the industry. On the horizontal x-axis list all the important features of a product/service that organizations try to compete for in the industry. Think of, for example, price, speed, reliability, ease of use, and so forth. On the vertical y-axis make a scale from low to high. Then draw various lines that show how you and your key competitors score on the various features. This should give you some detailed insights into how your product differs from theirs. It might also give you insights into gaps in the market. This is the case when all the lines that you draw are similar (showing that everyone is competing for the same thing).

**For finding ways to use your competitors in a smart way:** Brandenburger and Nalebuff's Cooperative game theory or 'Co-Opetition.' It presents five factors that you can use to make competition work for you:

1. **Players:** Merely becoming a player in an industry can already have value for others (for example because you increase competition, which is good for customers). Use this.

② **Added value:** Increase your added value by making others depend more on you than vice versa (for example by limiting supply to distributors).

③ **Rules:** You can benefit from changing the rules of the game by smart contracting (for example by giving early or late customers a reduced price) or by actively engaging in setting standards.

④ **Tactics:** By showing and hiding information you can trigger and influence competitors' reactions (for example by 'leaking' to the press or creating an atmosphere of exclusivity around your product).

⑤ **Scope:** You can benefit from combining or separating the various 'games' you play in different (parts of) industries (for example by providing complementary products to yours or using multiple brands).

These five 'PARTS' are quite difficult to understand and to use in practice. Yet, if you really understand them, they can be powerful ways to benefit from your competitors. Therefore, I recommend reading more about this model – for example in their book on 'Co-Opetition.'

# 5 Value proposition

The core of your strategy is your value proposition. It reflects what products, services, and added value you offer and how you offer this to your customers. When you map this element of your strategy, it is useful to take the following into account:

- Don't try to be complete when describing the value of your products or services. Focus on the essence. What features are most valuable?
- When you think about the value of your product or service to the customer, ask yourself *why* the customer buys your product and not another product, or a product from someone else.
- It can help to think about your value proposition in terms of *form* and *function.* The product, service, and way of offering are about the *form* of your offer (for example a book). The value is about the *function* (or 'use value') that your offer has for the customer (such as creating an understanding of strategy generation).
- It can be useful to make a systematic comparison of your products and services to those of competitors. Make a list of features and compare them. Where do you stand out?

## Questions to ask

| For understanding your *current* value proposition(s): | For developing *new* value proposition(s): |
|---|---|
| • What products or services do you offer? | • How can your products or services be made more valuable? |
| • What makes them different from those of others? | • What features can you improve, expand, or add? |
| • What value do they have for customers? | • What products, services, or features can be downgraded, simplified, or dropped? |
| • Why do people buy them? | |
| • What is special about them? | • What related or complementary products or services can you offer that your customers also need? |
| | • How can they be made more accessible? |

## Beyond-the-obvious exercise

You have your own idea about what is valuable about your products or services, but this is not necessarily the same as what your customers think. To increase your chances of seeing it their way, you can do a small role-playing exercise. Start by simply asking people to describe the value of the products or services they are selling. Then you ask them "So this is what you are selling. But what is your customer buying?" Tell them to take on the role of customer and then describe the value of your products or services again. The more realistic you make this, the better the description will be. So, encourage them to imitate a particular customer and literally use their voice or way of saying things. You will be amazed how people start seeing things quite differently in this way. Of course you can also do the exercise yourself instead of asking others.

# Step 2

## Inspirational checklist

To identify the value of your products and services, consider why people buy them or should buy them. For example, your (current or future) customers buy your products or services because these are…

- …low-priced, cheap to buy, or good value for money.
- …cheapest in terms of total cost of ownership or life-cycle costs.
- …easy to understand and use, convenient.
- …frequently offered, available everywhere.
- …fun, enjoyable to use or experience.
- …technologically sophisticated, using new technology.
- …well designed, beautiful, esthetic.
- …status enriching, making people feel better.
- …exclusive, available nowhere else, expensive.
- …used by many or important others, popular, trendy.
- …personalized, custom-made, tailored.
- …based on a good personal relationship, friendly.
- …simple, to the point, without frills, effort-reducing.
- …complete, advanced, thorough.
- …reliable, fault-free, solid, robust, risk-reducing.
- …modern, fashionable, up to date.
- …long-lasting, sustainable, durable.
- …environmentally friendly, efficient, green.

## Useful models

**For thinking about the value of your products and services in a simple way:** Sinek's Golden circle, which contains three concentric circles that express three dimensions of what you offer:

- **What** (outer circle): The products or services that you offer and that anyone can see and describe.
- **How** (inner circle): Things that make your products or services special compared to those of others.
- **Why** (core): The reason you do what you; the purpose and reason why your organization exists.

Sinek argues that the most successful organizations don't reason 'outside-in' (from what to how to why), but 'inside-out' (from why to how to what). Thus, they emphasize the purpose of what they are doing rather than the products and services they sell. Whatever order you will be using, this model is still useful to make you think about the purpose of your organization's products and services.

**For finding the generic type of value that you try to offer:** Treacy and Wiersema's Value disciplines. This model argues that an organization should try to excel at one of the following three types of value, while at the same time doing enough in the other two:

- **Operational excellence:** Smooth delivery; lowest costs in terms of money, time, effort, etc.
- **Product leadership:** Best product in terms of innovation, brand, quality, etc.
- **Customer intimacy:** Best total solution for each customer; customer service and attention, etc.

Treacy and Wiersema also argue that the most successful organizations in the world manage to excel in two dimensions. So, although it might be more difficult to excel in two, it might also be more rewarding to do so.

**For understanding the total product or service you offer and the various types of value it may have:** Kotler's Three levels of product:

- **Core product:** The product or service in the narrow sense. This describes the core benefit or the function of the product/service.
- **Actual product:** The distinctive product/service as the customer buys it. This goes beyond the functional characteristics of the product/service and includes styling, features, quality, and packaging.
- **Augmented product:** The product/service with everything it comes with, such as installation, guarantees, delivery, additional services, brand value.

**For generating ideas for a new value proposition:** Kim and Mauborgne's Blue Ocean 'Four actions framework.' It distinguishes four actions that you can use to develop a value proposition that is different from what is currently offered in the industry. When thinking about the value propositions currently offered (by you or by other companies), see which features you can:

- **Create** that the current industry does not offer.
- **Raise** well above the industry's standard.
- **Reduce** well below the industry's standard.
- **Eliminate** that the industry takes for granted.

This framework can be well used as a follow up of the Strategy canvas that we saw a couple of pages ago (page 77).

# 6 Revenue model

With the first five elements we have covered those parts of your strategy that reveal how your organization creates value. This sixth element reflects what you get in return for this, from whom, and in what form. When you map out your revenue model you should take the following into account:

- Although your customers might be the first you think of when it concerns payment, look at others as well. Basically, anyone who benefits from what you are offering is a possible candidate for paying you.
- Your revenue model needs to match your value proposition. This means that if you offer low value, you can't ask for a high price. But it also means that if you create high value, you should set a price consistent with that. By asking for too low a price, you confuse your customers.
- Don't easily reduce your price or rate. There is no way back. If necessary offer temporary reductions. Also, understand price sensitivity: Can you raise prices without a significant reduction in demand?
- Look at margin and volume. Both high-margin low-volume and low-margin high-volume strategies work.
- Think about more than money alone. Maybe someone cannot pay, but what else can they help you with? Information, access, resources, time, advice; anything with a value can be considered. In the end, others might want to pay for these.

## Questions to ask

| For capturing your current revenue model: | For developing or finding new revenue models: |
|---|---|
| • Where does your revenue come from? | • Can you change how customers pay, when, or for what? |
| • Which people or organizations pay? | • Who benefits but doesn't pay yet or not enough? Can you let them pay? |

- For what do they pay?

- How much do they pay?

- How, or in what form do they pay?

- Can you make your revenue less dependent on your efforts?

- Can you turn products into services and vice versa?

- What revenue streams should be dropped? Which ones are too complicated or don't bring enough?

## Beyond-the-obvious exercise

It is usually not very difficult to map out your current revenue model. There is a big chance that most of your revenue comes from customers and that you rely, for example, on a 'p times q' model (number of hours/items times the price per hour/item). A useful exercise for revealing other revenue generating options is drawing a *value network*. This is a picture showing how money and other resources flow between key players. Start by drawing all the important stakeholders on a sheet of paper. Next, using arrows, draw what value exchanges there are between them. Next to each arrow write what each player offers and what they get in return. In a balanced value network, all the players contribute *and* receive. The latter may be indirectly, though, through other players – as illustrated in the example below: Customers pay you for delivery services that a distributor offers. Once completed, the value network might reveal players that benefit more than they contribute. These are your potential sources of untapped revenue.

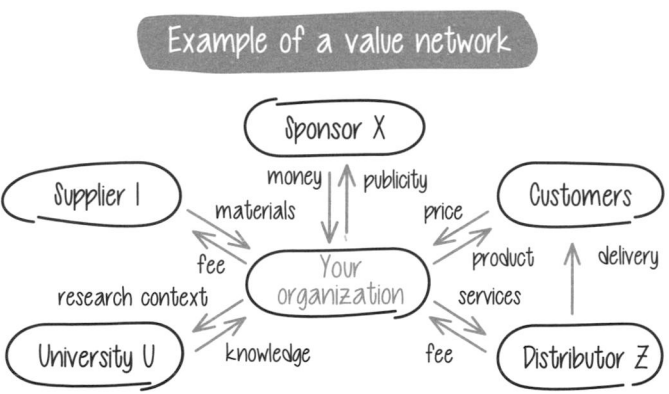

**Example of a value network**

83

## Inspirational checklist

To find new ways in which customers or others can pay, consider whether your revenue model could be based on...

- ...selling the product/service. The default for most products.
- ...bundled pricing. Sell products/services as a package deal.
- ...disaggregated pricing. Let people only pay for what they want or use.
- ...usage fees. Fee per click, minute, day, etc.
- ...renting or leasing. Fee for using a product/service for a given period.
- ...subscriptions. Receive a fixed fee per month or so.
- ...memberships. Fee for being a member plus getting free extras.
- ...vouchers and gift cards. Pay in advance, use the product/service later.
- ...freemium. Offer free and paid versions of the product.
- ...advertising. Free product, but advertisements to look at.
- ...licensing. Fee for using copyrights or patents.
- ...shares or crowd funding. Invest in potential future revenue.
- ...donors and sponsors. Voluntary payments with little return in favor.
- ...subsidies. Governments pay for jobs, sustainability, or innovation.
- ...brokerage. Fee per successful transaction.
- ...auctioning or reverse-auctioning. Let people bid.
- ...flexible pricing. Vary prices based on demand.
- ...barter. In kind payment or swapping goods.
- ...no-cure-no-pay (or less-pay). Customers only pay if satisfied.
- ...affiliation. Fee per new customer that is brought in.
- ...interest. Fee for loans or other forms of financing.
- ...razorblading. Offer a cheap product plus sell expensive supplies.

## Useful models

**For setting the right price:** Shapiro and Jackson's Pricing models, arguing there are three starting points for pricing that you can choose or combine:

1. **Cost-based:** Look at your costs and add a percentage to have a high enough margin.
2. **Competition-based:** Look at your competitors' prices and choose your own price accordingly.
3. **Value-based:** Assess how much your products or services are worth to customers.

**For exploring who might be willing to pay or contribute to your organization:** Freeman's Stakeholder map, showing the (potential) stakeholders of the organization:

1. **Primary stakeholders** such as customers, suppliers, complementors, financers, employees, neighbors, shareholders, or communities.
2. **Secondary stakeholders** such as governments, competitors, consumer advocate groups, media, education institute, special interest groups, journalists, or analysts.

(See also 'Partners' on page 66).

**For understanding earnings per customer or per transaction and for focusing on the most valuable ones:** The Pareto principle or 80-20 rule, providing evidence that in most cases a small group of customers or transactions is responsible for the majority of earnings/profits, while the rest only contributes marginally. Check whether this is also the case for your organization and whether you should perhaps focus more on the upper 20% and say goodbye to other customers.

# 7 Risks & costs

Your strategy doesn't only come with revenue – it also involves risks and costs. So, when mapping your strategy, you also want to identify the financial, social, and other risks and costs your bear. When mapping this, you want to take the following into account:

- Look at the relation with your revenue model and value proposition to check whether things that involve risks and costs add sufficient value. So, for each activity or element of your strategy compare how much value they add and how much costs and risks are involved.
- There often is a trade-off between costs and risks. Hiring freelancers, for example, reduces risks, but it can also increase variable costs. The best advice is to look for ways to reduce both.
- Cash is king. Many organizations suffer liquidity problems – especially when they start becoming successful and start growing. So, make sure you are actively managing your cash.
- To limit risks and costs, try to use principles from 'bootstrapping:' Don't buy what you can rent, don't rent what you can barter for,

don't barter for what you can borrow, don't borrow what you can get for free.

- Do as expert entrepreneurs do: Make investments based on what you can afford to lose instead of based on calculations of what you might earn.

## Questions to ask

| For assessing your *current* costs and risks: | For *diminishing* your costs and risks in the future: |
|---|---|
| • For each other element: What risks and costs and are associated with it? | • Can you eliminate, reduce, or share some costs or risks? |
| • How large are these risks and costs and who bears them? | • Can you hedge or neutralize them by other elements of your strategy? |
| • Which ones are necessary and which ones can be avoided? | • Can you transfer or outsource them to someone else? |
| • What can you afford to invest or lose? | • Can you postpone costs, or make them variable instead of fixed? |
| • Is this more or less than you currently do? | • Can you benefit from increasing some of the risks or costs you bear? |

## Beyond-the-obvious exercises

It is relatively easy to see *what* costs and revenue you have. It is harder to see, though, *when* and *where* they occur. There are two exercises you can do to gain these insights. The simplest one is drawing a line chart of how your overall revenue and costs have developed over the past years. Depending on the kind of organization you have, it might be most useful to do this by year, quartile, or month. This chart gives you an insight into the level of your revenue and costs and *when* they occur.

If you want more in-depth insights into *where* costs and revenues are made, you should link them to the key activities of your organization.

This will show you whether the activities on which you spend most time or money are also the ones which have the most added value for the customer. You can do this through the following three steps:

1. Make a list of the key primary and secondary activities of your organization. Primary activities are those that contribute directly to your products/services, such as production, logistics, or sales. Secondary activities are your overheads. Examples are finance, human resource management, and marketing. The more refined you make your list of activities, the more refined your insight will be.

2. Map out the percentage of your total number of hours spent or of the total costs each activity is responsible for. This shows you where you spend your time and money.

3. Judge how much added value each activity has for your customer. Judge whether the time or money you spend on a particular activity is in balance with the added value it has for the customer.

This exercise may show you, for example, that you spend 20% of your time or budget on refining the looks of your webpage or on optimizing the performance of your product, whereas these activities have only little value for the customer. As such, it shows you where unnecessary costs are made.

## Inspirational checklist
To diminish the costs or risks that the organization bears, consider whether and how you can...
- ...make customers pay a part or everything in advance.
- ...delay payments to suppliers so that you keep your cash.
- ...do the opposite: pay suppliers early if you can get discounts.
- ...sell something before actually making it.
- ...share risks and costs by making others co-owners.
- ...outsource activities or hire freelancers.
- ...focus on what you really need, not more.
- ...ask others for access to their resources rather than buying them.
- ...make others commit before you take action.
- ...standardize or simplify products or services.
- ...share capacity or capabilities with others.
- ...reduce or reuse waste, materials, space, and energy.
- ...fail small and quickly through trial and error.
- ...make things mobile, e.g. through telecommuting.

- ...buy second hand or barter goods and services.
- ...clean up unnecessary assets and paperwork.
- ...keep things flexible and keep actions reversible as much as possible.
- ...stage projects and abandon them when needed.
- ...invest only what you can afford to lose.
- ...work on alternative products/services in parallel.

## Useful models

**For deciding what you should do yourself and what you should outsource to others:** Williamson's Transaction cost theory. Transaction costs are all the costs involved in making an exchange. These include costs to:

- Search and check information needed for a decision.
- Negotiate with and convince people to work for you.
- Monitor and control whether one does as agreed.

If external transaction costs are higher, you should do things yourself; if internal costs are higher, outsource.

**For reducing waste and becoming more efficient:** Toyota's Lean manufacturing approach. It aims at reducing seven types of waste:

- **Transportation:** No unnecessary movements that incur damage, loss, delay, etc.
- **Inventory:** No unneeded stock or work-in-progress.
- **Motion:** No unneeded motions. They cause exhaustion, wear and tear, etc.
- **Waiting:** No unnecessary delays.
- **Over-performing:** No unneeded specs, quality, etc.
- **Over-production:** Don't make more than ordered.
- **Defects:** Limit defects at any stage.

**For benchmarking or applying a professional approach to risk management:** The ISO 31000 standard. This internationally recognized family of standards provides a lot of information about how to identify, assess, avoid, accept, change, share, or retain risks. If you want to manage your risks in a professional manner, or if you want to find out how well you are already doing this, you should look up this ISO standard and learn from it.

**For learning more about how to manage and reduce risks, waste, and costs:** A whole family of risk, waste, and cost-reduction approaches. Examples are Six sigma, Lean six sigma, Total quality management, the 5S method, Continuous improvement, or Value engineering. Just look them up for more information.

# 8 Values & goals

After mapping out the first seven elements you have a good sense of how your organization creates value and what it gets in return. The eighth element that is crucial in any strategy are your values and goals. These reflect what is important for the organization and where it should go in the future. When mapping this element you should take the following into account:

- Without values or goals an organization might easily drift, meander, or stagnate. On the other hand, too strict goals and values might make it dogmatic and blind. Therefore balance is needed.
- Values and goals might be noble, such as solving poverty in the world. They can also be more mundane, though, such as a 5% yearly growth.
- Financial goals easily suppress other goals. Beware and regularly check which ones take the lead so that the organization keeps on track with what it is really aiming for.
- Values and goals need not always be SMART (specific, measurable, achievable, relevant, and time-bound). They might be more open and uncrystallized, as long as they are functional for the organization.
- The organization's formal and written values and goals might be different from the informal, factual values and goals that appear in decision-making and in what the organization actually does.

# Step 2

## Questions to ask

| For explicating *actual* values and goals as they appear in actions and decisions: | For explicating *desired* values and goals for the future: |
| --- | --- |
| • What criteria have been most decisive in key decisions so far? | • What is really important for the organization? Why was it founded? |
| • What has been achieved in the past three years? | • Who are the organization's main stakeholders? What should the organization do for them? |
| • If the organization continues what it is doing, where will it end up? | • What long-term goals or ambitions would create excitement? |
| • How would employees or outsiders describe the organization's values and goals? | • What is the right thing to do for the organization? How can it make a better impact? |
| • Are official values and goals shared throughout the organization? | • What values or goals are hindering progress and should be adjusted? |

## Beyond-the-obvious exercise

In many organizations it is quite clear what the official values and goals are. They are often written down in statements or reports and you often find them on the organization's webpage. The organization's *actual* values and goals as they appear in people's decisions and actions, though, are much harder to identify. Since these show what actually drives the organization you want to understand these too. There is a simple exercise to do this. The basic idea is that you look at a number of important or recent decisions or actions and identify the implicit or explicit criteria that were used there. More specifically you could look at the criteria used...

- ...in the three most recent or largest investments.
- ...in the three most recent or important strategic decisions.
- ...to assess the performance of people or departments.

This exercise might reveal, for example, that the most important criterion used is cost-reduction. And this might be quite different to what the organization's official values and goals say.

## Inspirational checklist

To identify the organization's values and goals, consider whether it is important that the organization...

- ...grows fast and becomes large.
- ...remains small and personal.
- ...has a strong international presence.
- ...is profitable or makes a lot of money.
- ...makes your shareholders or owners happy.
- ...serves a particular group of customers.
- ...solves an important and pressing problem.
- ...is a fun and energizing place to work.
- ...makes a difference to this world.
- ...is known for its ... (fill in yourself).
- ...is the most innovative of its kind.
- ...has the most satisfied customers.
- ...is bought by another organization.
- ...is there to stay in the long run.
- ...has the best reputation in the industry.
- ...changes the world or makes it a better place.
- ...is efficient and sustainable.

## Useful models

**For effectively expressing the organization's values and goals:**
The distinction between vision, mission, key values, and objectives:

1. **Vision:** Your aspirations or dreams for the future. A good vision is challenging and it should not yet be entirely clear how you could achieve it. In that way it creates a creative tension between where you are now and where you want to be.
2. **Mission:** What kind of organization you want to be on your way towards this vision. A good mission expresses who your organization's main stakeholders are and what you do for them.
3. **Key values:** What you find important. When used effectively, values are used as the basis for the organization's actions and decisions. They provide a stable ground for everyday and the longer term.
4. **Objectives:** What you want to achieve. Good objectives are SMART: Specific, measurable, achievable, relevant, and time-bound.

**For selecting which stakeholders the organization will focus on:** Mitchell et al.'s Stakeholder salience model in which they define three characteristics that are important in selecting stakeholders:

1. **Power:** You cannot do without them.
2. **Urgency:** They have urgent needs.
3. **Legitimacy:** You find them important.

The more of these characteristics a particular party has, the more likely it is an important stakeholder for your organization. Yet, selecting them remains a choice.

**For understanding three types of purposes for organizations:** the Triple bottom line or 3Ps of performance evaluation and sustainability:

1. **Profit,** or the economic impact of an organization. This has long been seen as the single most important type of impact, especially for profit-oriented businesses: making money.
2. **People,** or the organization's social impact. This dimension concerns the positive and negative impact of an organization on its employees, communities, or any other type of stakeholder.
3. **Planet,** or the organization's ecological impact. This concerns the positive or negative environmental impact of the organization.

Organizations make all three types of impact. However, one can deliberately focus or prioritize one above the other.

**For a pragmatic approach to deciding what is right or wrong:** Texas Instruments' guidelines for ethical decision-making:
- Is the action legal? If no, stop immediately.
- Does it comply with our values? If it does not, stop.
- If you do it would you feel bad? If so, stop.
- How would this look in the newspaper? Bad? Stop.
- If you know it's wrong don't do it.
- If you are not sure, ask until you get an answer.

**For making sure that expressed goals and values are also realized:** the Pyramid of purpose, which distinguishes four levels or questions for strategy execution:

1. Why are we doing what we are doing?
2. What do we need to do in order to achieve it?
3. How exactly are we going to do it?
4. Who or what is going to make sure it is done?

# 9 Organizational climate

Next to identifying the values and goals that drive the organization, you also need to understand the organization itself. Therefore, the next step is to map out the organizational climate – the structure and culture that are characteristic for the organization. When doing so, you should take notice of the following:

- Culture and structure are strongly related. They both reflect the organizational climate and there is no point in spending a lot of time in trying to separate them.
- Look both at the formal and the informal structure and culture. If these are very different, this can be a problem. If so, decide which one needs to be changed.
- There is no one best organizational climate that works in all organizations. What is important, though, is that it matches your strategy. Therefore, carefully look at what culture and structure suit your strategy – and vice versa.
- Ask newcomers and people from outside your organization how they would characterize its culture. These people might see this differently (and better) from you.

# Step 2

## Questions to ask

| For assessing the *current* organizational climate: | For *changing and improving* the organizational climate: |
| --- | --- |
| • How precisely and rigidly are tasks defined and how are they divided? | • What is the main thing that needs to be improved in terms of the questions in the left column? |
| • How is power divided and used and who is the most powerful? | • What would the ideal culture or structure look like if you could build the organization from scratch? |
| • How does communication take place? Who communicates with whom and about what? | |
| • What is characteristic of the organization? | • What organization is a role model for yours? |
| • What kind of symbols, rituals, or stories are frequently used? | • What would be the first thing to drop or change about the organization's structure or culture? |

## Beyond-the-obvious exercise

There might be all kinds of assumptions about your organization's climate. Employees might say, for example, that the organization is particularly innovative, or that it is like a big family. But is this really so? To break out of these assumptions, you can do the following exercise. The core idea of this exercise is that you make people look at their organization in an unusual manner by using metaphors. To get a good sense of the organizational climate, ask them one or more of the following questions:

- If our organization was an animal, it would be a ... because ...
- If our organization was a food, it would be ... because ...
- If our organization was a sport, it would be ... because ...
- If our organization was a TV show, it would be ... because ...
- If our organization was a color, it would be ... because ...

You can also use other metaphors such as a season, a plant, type of building, car model, toy, type of furniture, and so on. Make sure that people do not just name the animal, food, etc. but also explain why.

## Inspirational checklist

To identify ways to improve the organizational climate, consider whether and how you can...

- ...give people more autonomy and responsibility.
- ...make people work and think more entrepreneurially.
- ...create an atmosphere in which failure is allowed.
- ...rely less on analysis and more on action.
- ...encourage people to accept and act under uncertainty.
- ...allocate time and resources for exploration.
- ...combine the short term with the long term.
- ...do only what is urgent and/or important.
- ...understand and focus on what customers really want.
- ...create a flexible and learning organization.
- ...foster a sense of reality among all the people.
- ...keep procedures, forms, and spreadsheets simple.
- ...avoid complex structures with many layers.
- ...create small units in which people know each other.
- ...foster collaboration within and between units.
- ...realize a large extent of transparency and openness.
- ...motivate people to give everything they can.
- ...work towards goals and values that matter to people.
- ...challenge people to go beyond the status-quo.
- ...get rid of disturbing or underperforming people.
- ...clean up the entire organization at least once a year.

## Useful models

**For understanding the main elements of the organizational climate:** Johnson's Cultural web, containing six elements of the organization's culture:

- **Stories:** The things from the past people talk about.
- **Symbols:** Visual representations such as logos, buildings, and dress code.
- **Rituals and routines:** Habits and procedures showing how people are expected to behave.
- **Organizational structure:** The way tasks are divided and coordinated in the organization.

- **Control systems:** Financial, monitoring, and other systems for controlling the organization.
- **Power structures:** The real way power is divided, showing who has most influence on decisions.

**For a quick insight into the performance orientation of the organizational climate:** Birkinshaw and Gibson's four organizational contexts. Based on two dimensions – social support and performance management – they distinguish four types of organizational contexts:

1. **Low performance:** Low social support, low performance management.
2. **High performance:** High social support, high performance management.
3. **Burnout:** Low social support, high performance management.
4. **Country club:** High social support, low performance management.

As the name suggests, the second context generally leads to the best performance. It reflects an organization that is both challenging and supportive. You can use this model to assess whether your organizational climate fosters high performance or not.

**For assessing the culture of your organization:** The Organizational Culture Assessment Instrument (OCAI), which distinguishes four types of culture, characterized by the following keywords:
- **Clan culture:** Pleasant, cohesive, loyalty, moral, long-term relationships, friendly.
- **Adhocracy culture:** Entrepreneurial, flexible, innovative, risk-taking, creative, change.
- **Market culture:** Competitive, results-oriented, hard-working, productive, performance.
- **Hierarchy culture:** Formalized and structured, rule-based, efficient, procedural, stability.

As you can already infer from the keywords, each culture has its advantages and disadvantages. A clan culture, for example, supports collaboration, while a market culture supports hard work. You can use this model to assess whether the culture of your organization matches its strategy of whether a change in culture is needed.

**For understanding the maturity or growth-stage of the organization:** Greiner's Growth model, which distinguishes six stages of development:

① **Creativity:** Start-up, informal small team, innovation, *but* no clear leader and direction.

② **Direction:** Planning, setting goals, single leader manages all, *but* lacks time and overview.

③ **Delegation:** Managers take over some tasks of the leader, *but* fragmentation looms.

④ **Coordination:** Reorganization, clearer structure, *but* increasing bureaucracy.

⑤ **Collaboration:** Coherence, team-work, human relations, *but* internal growth limits reached.

⑥ **Alliances:** External growth, alliances, mergers, acquisitions, *but* lack of creativity may occur.

Knowing at what stage your organization is helps you understanding the particular strengths and weaknesses of your organizational climate and what it may take to grow further.

# 10 Trends & uncertainties

So far we have looked at the organization and its immediate surroundings – its partners, customers, and competitors. But also the broader environment is important for strategy generation. Therefore, as a last step, you should also pay attention to the trends and uncertainties in the organization's environment. When you map these, take the following into account:

- Don't aim for long lists of factors, trends, events, etc. Rather, focus on the most essential ones. Also, rather than just mentioning them, make explicit what they mean for your organization.
- Be aware that any trend or uncertainty in your environment also affects your competitors. Therefore, a trend that looks an opportunity could be a threat if competitors can better handle it. The same applies to threats; if you can handle them better than competitors, they are opportunities.
- Any trend or uncertainty that you can observe and name reflects what Peter Drucker (a famous management guru) has called "the future that already happened." Don't fall into the trap where you start thinking that you can actually predict the future.
- Mind gradual changes. They are easily overlooked because you get used to them. Therefore, they require deliberate and careful observation.

# Step 2

## Questions to ask

| For assessing *current* trends and uncertainties: | For finding ways to *respond* to them: |
|---|---|
| • What important trends are going on in the industry and society? | • Can you find a way to benefit more from what goes on? |
| • Which ones can you better deal with than competitors? And vice versa? | • Can you move to a more favorable environment? |
| • What will definitely change in the next few years? | • Can you make the organization less dependent on the trends and uncertainties it faces? |
| • Which are the biggest uncertainties the organization faces? | • Can you exploit opportunities or turn a threat into an opportunity? |
| • How uncertain is the environment of your organization? How dynamic and complex is it? | • What does it take to exploit the opportunity? Do you have it or can you easily develop it? |

## Beyond-the-obvious exercise

There is a good chance that mapping out trends and uncertainties just leads to general trends such as 'aging' or 'globalization.' These may be important, but you also want to go more in depth. One way to do this was already partially mentioned in Chapter 3. The first tactic to reveal the urgency of new strategy ("Ask whether the organization will still exist in five years," see page 47) is also a good starting point for revealing trends and uncertainties. So, for this exercise you start by asking whether the organization will still exist in five years if it would just continue doing what it does today. If the answer to this question is "no," your follow-up questions are "Why not?" and "What are the important factors in your environment that cause you to remain unchanged?"

## Inspirational checklist

To identify the relevant trends and uncertainties for the organization, consider the positive and negative consequences of triggers such as...

- ...entry, exit, mergers, splitting, acquisitions, and alliances of competitors, suppliers or customers.
- ...changes in people's habits, needs, or preferences.
- ...changes in the composition of the population.
- ...one technology taking over another technology.
- ...developments in adjacent industries.
- ...political events, taxes, subsidies, laws, or regulations that change the rules of the game.
- ...the economy going up and down.
- ...local or global disasters or other crises.
- ...'megatrends' such as globalization, power redistribution, urbanization, climate change, aging, increased interconnectivity, and mobility.
- ...changes in the norms about what is right and wrong.
- ...maturation and commoditization of current markets.
- ...opinions of opinion leaders, media, or the public.
- ...availability and distribution of money, materials, skilled people, information, or other resources.
- ...changing online or offline infrastructure.

## Useful models

**For identifying different types of trends in your environment:**
The PESTLE analysis (or one of its at least 15 variants such as PEST, DESTEP, or STEEPLE). This divides the analysis of your environment into six categories:

- **Political** factors such as taxes, subsidies, trade barriers, and the political regime you're in.
- **Economic** factors such as the interest rate, economic growth, availability of capital, or exchange rates.
- **Social** factors such as demographics, population growth, aging, people's attitudes and values.
- **Technological** factors such as IT, automation, R&D, inventions, or technology becoming outdated.
- **Legal** factors such as civil law, criminal law, banking law, computer law, competition law, or alcohol law.
- **Environmental** factors such as climate and climate change, the weather, landscape, or natural resources.

For understanding the stage of your industry: The industry life cycle. According to this model every industry moves through various stages:

1. **Introduction:** A few initial versions of a new product or service; early adopters as customers.
2. **Growth:** Increasing competition, more variants of products/services; early majority as customers.
3. **Maturity:** Standardization of products/services, focus on price, shakeout with few strong competitors. Late majority as customers.
4. **Decline:** Products/services becoming obsolete, decreasing prices, competitors withdrawing, falling demand, and 'laggards' as customers.

Knowing which stage you are at helps you better understand the nature and dynamics of your industry.

For understanding the degree of uncertainty you face: The environmental uncertainty matrix. Based on two dimensions – degree of change and degree of complexity – this matrix defines four types of environments:

1. **Stable and simple:** Low uncertainty because changes are small and concern only a few factors in the environment.
2. **Stable and complex:** Low/medium uncertainty. Although many factors are relevant, they can be understood because they hardly change.
3. **Unstable and simple:** Medium/high uncertainty. Only a small number of factors, but they change frequently and in an unpredictable way.
4. **Unstable and complex:** High uncertainty. Many factors to take into account that change frequently. Almost impossible to analyze.

Once you know which quadrant your organization is in, this makes you aware of the uncertainty of your environment. The more uncertain, the less you should rely on information and analysis, and the more on taking control.

For creating a more advanced insight in the interplay of trends and uncertainties and what they could mean for the organization: Scenario planning. There are plenty of different approaches, but they usually include variations of the following steps:

1. Scope the question and the time horizon of the scenario project.
2. Identify and rank the most important trends and uncertainties.
3. Bring them together in a sensible framework, for example by clustering them or projecting them in a two-by-two matrix.
4. Develop two to four scenarios based on the framework.
5. Write narratives for each scenario. Make them as realistic as possible by including dynamics, players, conflicts, story lines, and titles.
6. Reflect on the outcomes. Consider the plausibility, relevance and implications of the scenarios.

Note that the purpose of scenario planning is not to predict the future or find the most likely scenario. Instead, you are constructing possible scenarios, thereby increasing your awareness of possible futures.

# The **four** examples

On the next few pages you will find the completed Strategy Sketches of our four examples. I am not saying these are perfect examples, or even particularly good ones. They just show you the kind of information that is typically mentioned in this second step of the strategy generation process. When you have a look at these four sketches, you will get quite a good sense of what the strategies of these four organizations look like. You might also see inconsistencies, questions, or problems, but that is also quite common – if the sketches were perfect, there would be no reason to engage in strategy generation in the first place!

See Strategy Sketches on the next page

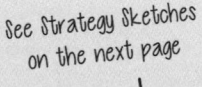

## Macman

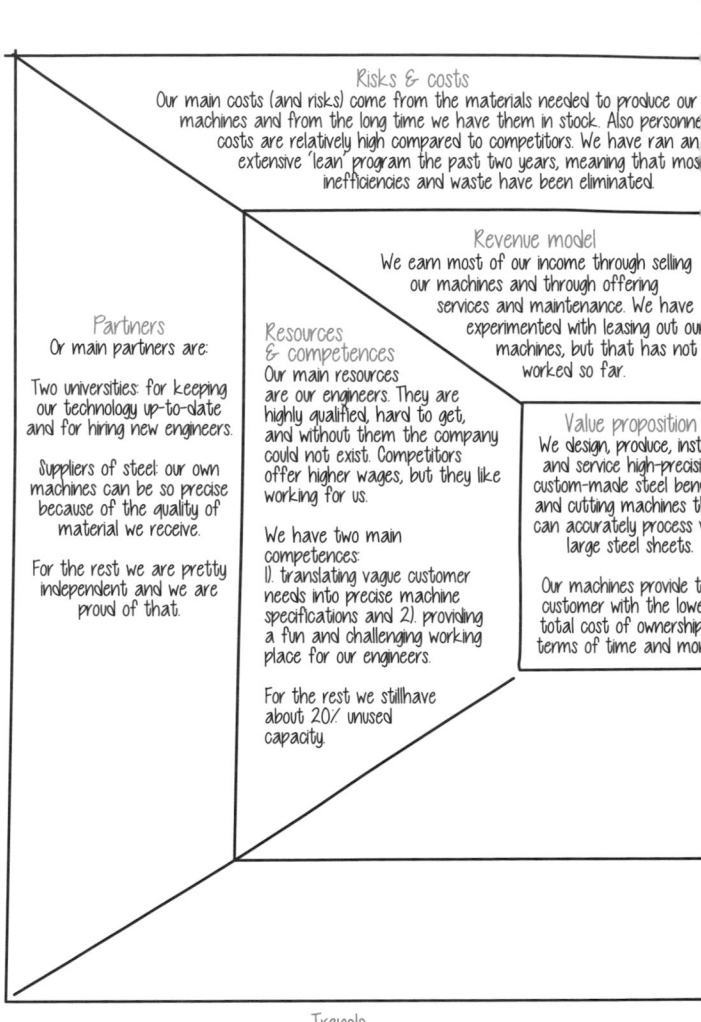

**Risks & costs**
Our main costs (and risks) come from the materials needed to produce our machines and from the long time we have them in stock. Also personne costs are relatively high compared to competitors. We have ran an extensive 'lean' program the past two years, meaning that mos inefficiencies and waste have been eliminated.

**Revenue model**
We earn most of our income through selling our machines and through offering services and maintenance. We have experimented with leasing out ou machines, but that has not worked so far.

**Partners**
Or main partners are:

Two universities: for keeping our technology up-to-date and for hiring new engineers.

Suppliers of steel: our own machines can be so precise because of the quality of material we receive.

For the rest we are pretty independent and we are proud of that.

**Resources & competences**
Our main resources are our engineers. They are highly qualified, hard to get, and without them the company could not exist. Competitors offer higher wages, but they like working for us.

We have two main competences:
1). translating vague customer needs into precise machine specifications and 2). providing a fun and challenging working place for our engineers.

For the rest we stillhave about 20% unused capacity.

**Value proposition**
We design, produce, inst and service high-precisi custom-made steel ben and cutting machines t can accurately process large steel sheets.

Our machines provide t customer with the lowe total cost of ownership terms of time and mo

**Trends**
A main threat comes from China, where they are increasingly able to produce with high accuracy – at low cost. Increasing steel prices are worrisome too. Weapons industry is attractive and growing, but we say we don't want this...

## Uncertainties

Plastics seems to grow but it is unclear whether we are able to produce machines for that. Not so many uncertainties it seems; we are in a pretty stable industry. At least so far.

## Competitors

We have plenty of competitors.

Three in Europe, offering a similar quality level. Our main advantage is the personal relationship we have with customers, but we're too expensive.

Competition mainly came from the US so far, but three new Chinese competitors have entered the market recently.

We mostly compete with Company X for new orders. To be honest, they are just as good as we but offer lower prices.

## Customers & needs

Our main customers are 2 large high-precision machine manufacturers in Europe that require steel cutting and bending machines.

Few irregular other customers

The customers of our customers are manufacturers of medical precision instruments. They need extremely reliable and accurate equipment.

## ues & goals

re are a couple of things
really find important:
though we could very well, we don't
rve the weapon industry.
r employees should be modest, like their
rk, and listen to customers.
e don't need to grow, but we do want to keep our current size.

## Organizational climate

The climate of our organization can be best characterized as hard-
orking, loyal, high-tech, and fun. We lack an entrepreneurial spirit though,
which is why we are not good at coming up with new ideas.

# Hospicare

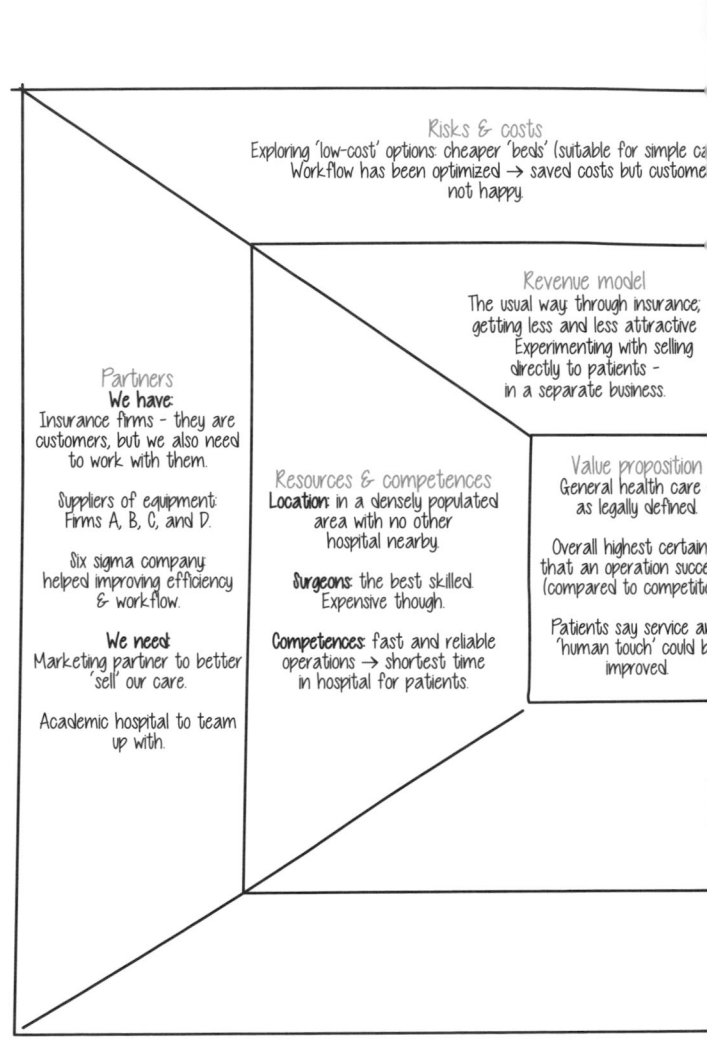

**Risks & costs**
Exploring 'low-cost' options: cheaper 'beds' (suitable for simple ca...
Workflow has been optimized → saved costs but custome...
not happy.

**Revenue model**
The usual way: through insurance;
getting less and less attractive
Experimenting with selling
directly to patients -
in a separate business.

**Partners**
**We have:**
Insurance firms - they are
customers, but we also need
to work with them.

Suppliers of equipment:
Firms A, B, C, and D.

Six sigma company:
helped improving efficiency
& workflow.

**We need:**
Marketing partner to better
'sell' our care.

Academic hospital to team
up with.

**Resources & competences**
**Location:** in a densely populated
area with no other
hospital nearby.

**Surgeons:** the best skilled.
Expensive though.

**Competences:** fast and reliable
operations → shortest time
in hospital for patients.

**Value proposition**
General health care ...
as legally defined.

Overall highest certain...
that an operation succe...
(compared to competit...

Patients say service a...
'human touch' could b...
improved.

**Trends**
Upcoming commercial health providers, operating outside the normal circuit
Increased specialization.

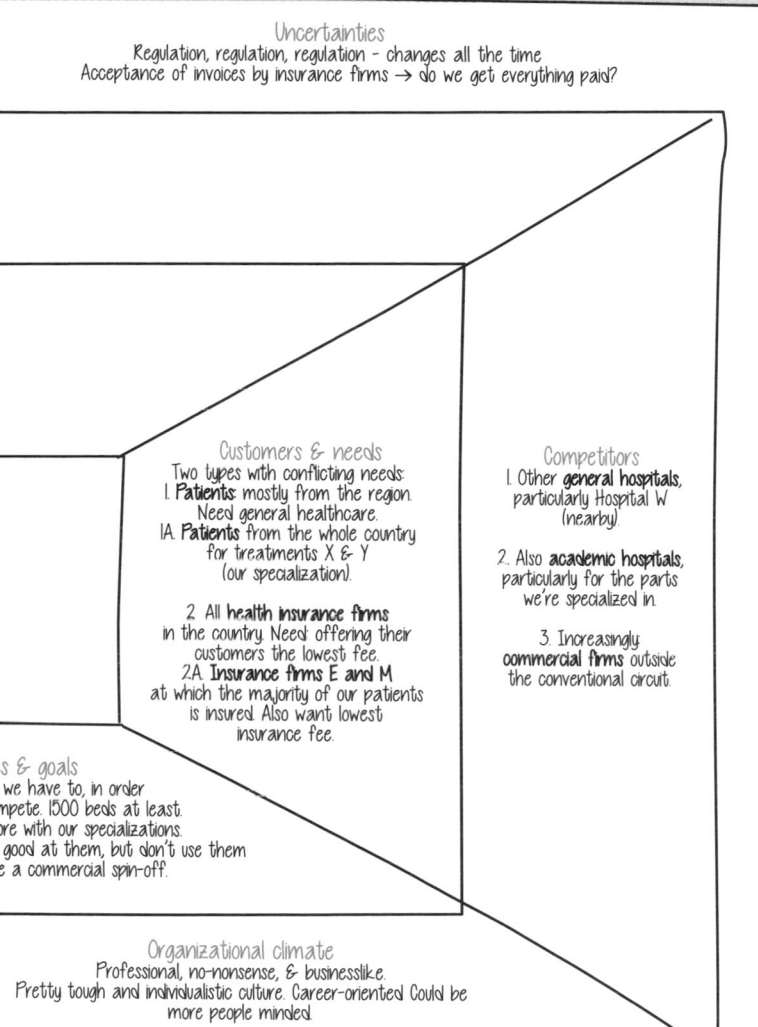

**Uncertainties**
Regulation, regulation, regulation - changes all the time
Acceptance of invoices by insurance firms → do we get everything paid?

**Customers & needs**
Two types with conflicting needs:
1. **Patients** mostly from the region.
   Need general healthcare.
1A. **Patients** from the whole country
   for treatments X & Y
   (our specialization).

2. All **health insurance firms**
in the country. Need offering their
   customers the lowest fee.
2A. **Insurance firms E and M**
at which the majority of our patients
is insured. Also want lowest
insurance fee.

**Competitors**
1. Other **general hospitals**,
particularly Hospital W
(nearby).

2. Also **academic hospitals**,
particularly for the parts
we're specialized in.

3. Increasingly:
**commercial firms** outside
the conventional circuit.

**...es & goals**
..., we have to, in order
...ompete. 1500 beds at least.
...nore with our specializations.
...e good at them, but don't use them
...te a commercial spin-off.

**Organizational climate**
Professional, no-nonsense, & businesslike.
Pretty tough and individualistic culture. Career-oriented. Could be
more people minded.

105

GoforIT

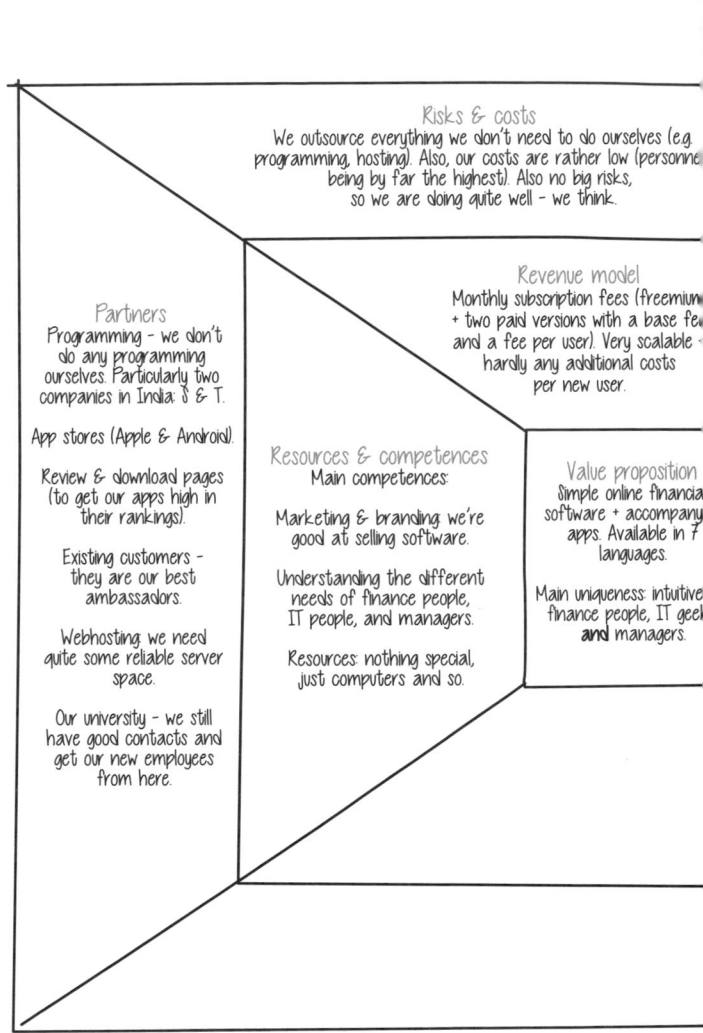

**Risks & costs**
We outsource everything we don't need to do ourselves (e.g. programming, hosting). Also, our costs are rather low (personnel being by far the highest). Also no big risks, so we are doing quite well - we think.

**Revenue model**
Monthly subscription fees (freemium + two paid versions with a base fee and a fee per user). Very scalable - hardly any additional costs per new user.

**Partners**
Programming - we don't do any programming ourselves. Particularly two companies in India: S & T.

App stores (Apple & Android).

Review & download pages (to get our apps high in their rankings).

Existing customers - they are our best ambassadors.

Webhosting we need quite some reliable server space.

Our university - we still have good contacts and get our new employees from here.

**Resources & competences**
Main competences:

Marketing & branding: we're good at selling software.

Understanding the different needs of finance people, IT people, and managers.

Resources: nothing special, just computers and so.

**Value proposition**
Simple online financial software + accompanying apps. Available in 7 languages.

Main uniqueness: intuitive finance people, IT geeks **and** managers.

**Trends**
Upcoming free and ad-based alternatives. Might threaten our position. Also, increased privacy and security awareness. Could be good or bad for us. Decreasing willingness to pay. People think everything in software is for free!

## Uncertainties

How long can we still rely on our technology? It can be easily copied by others. We're relying on our brand, but that is a bit shaky.

## Customers & needs

Small businesses across the globe (5-50 employees).

So far mainly in Latin-America, Southern Europe, and Australia.

Within these companies:
**Users**: financial departments
**Decision-makers**: owner/CEO
**Key influencer**: IT department

## Competitors
Plenty.

Providers of free financial software. (not really good, but customers consider this first).

Providers of paid financial software. (more threatening, but they are still quite conventional).

Closest to what we do: Companies R, T, and Z. Customers choose for them too, and their software is a bit comparable.

## es & goals

sted in the top 10 of at least 'fast growing ventures' list.
more systematic attention to strategy – e than the intuitive approach so far.
a foothold in Germany – a challenge since our ware deviates from the 'normal'.

## Organizational climate

Very entrepreneurial and creative – but also messy. We are a bunch of enthusiasts, but we probably need more structure if we want to grow further.

Comcom

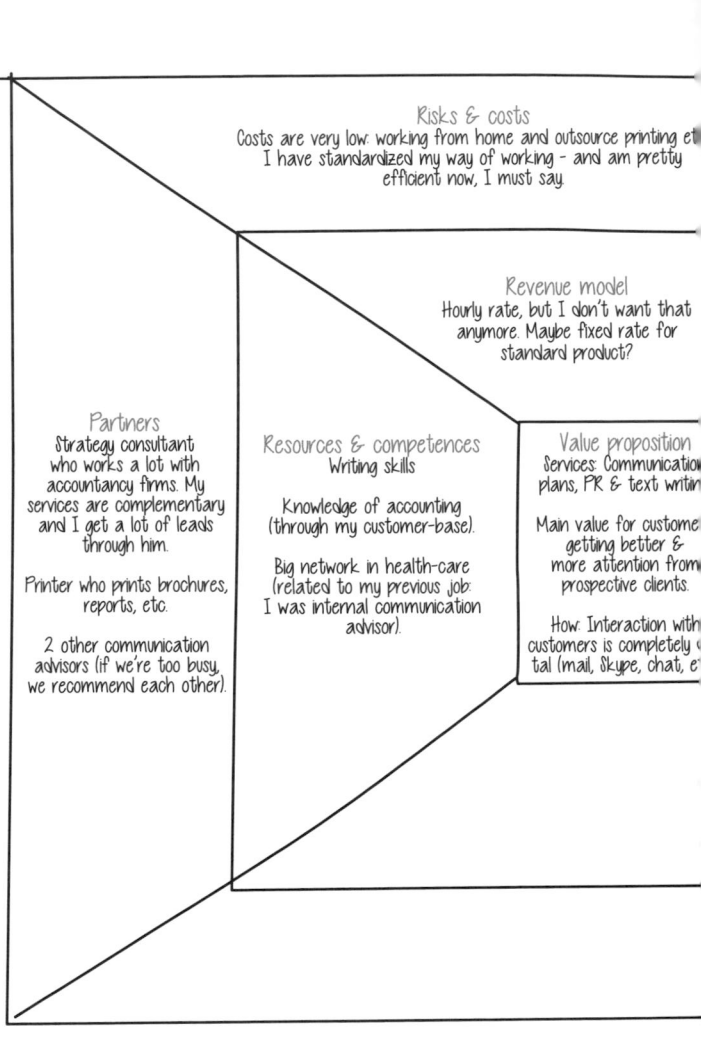

**Risks & costs**
Costs are very low: working from home and outsource printing et[...]
I have standardized my way of working - and am pretty
efficient now, I must say.

**Revenue model**
Hourly rate, but I don't want that
anymore. Maybe fixed rate for
standard product?

**Partners**
Strategy consultant
who works a lot with
accountancy firms. My
services are complementary
and I get a lot of leads
through him.

Printer who prints brochures,
reports, etc.

2 other communication
advisors (if we're too busy,
we recommend each other).

**Resources & competences**
Writing skills

Knowledge of accounting
(through my customer-base).

Big network in health-care
(related to my previous job:
I was internal communication
advisor).

**Value proposition**
Services: Communicatio[...]
plans, PR & text writin[...]

Main value for custome[...]
getting better &
more attention from
prospective clients.

How: Interaction with
customers is completely [...]
tal (mail, Skype, chat, e[...]

**Trends**
Price competition - freelance competitors ruin the market by asking ridiculously low rates.

## Uncertainties
Can I keep my current customers?? They are asking me to reduce prices al the time...
What will be a profitable niche? I have contacts in the restaurant business,
but will this fly?

## Customers & needs
For some reason mainly small to
medium-sized accountancy firms
(60-70% of turnover).

They need to show how they are
different from their competitors
(exactly what I need myself as well...).

## Competitors
Many many other
communication advisors.
They do more or less the
same (in the same country).

Marketing companies:
can offer more than just
communication (also strategy,
not my strong point).

## es & goals
nt to stay independent
freelancer.
nt (and need) more income:
ase revenues with at least 20% (soon).
n't want to work more. 50 hours is enough.
m: **a food blog or website read by thousands of people.**

## Organizational climate
Not much of an organization - just on my own.
I want to work digitally (keeps things flexible)
Need a better work-life balance - the job is starting to
be no fun anymore.

# Stepping back for a moment

Now that we have gone through the entire Strategy Sketch and have seen a variety of tools, this is a good moment to hold back for a second to look at what we have seen so far and what we can do with it already.

## A brief summary of what we have seen so far

We are about halfway through the book, and this is what we have seen so far:

1 A definition of strategy as a unique way of sustainable value creation.

2 Definitions and explanations of the ten most important elements of strategy.

3 The Strategy Sketch: A simple visual tool that integrates these elements onto a single sheet of paper in a coherent and systematic way.

4 Various activation tactics to make your key stakeholders ready to engage in strategy generation.

5 A set of questions to ask, beyond-the-obvious exercises, inspirational checklists, and useful models that help you to map out your current strategy and generate ideas for new strategy.

6 Four examples of Strategy Sketches covering all ten elements for our four organizations.

These tools complete the strategy mapping step of the strategy generation process. Furthermore, by providing a variety of suggestions on how to develop new strategy, these tools facilitate the third step - innovating strategy too. While the remainder of this book completes the full strategy generation process, you might want to stick to what we have seen so far - or at least for now. If you choose for this, you should have a look at the fast and frugal approach to strategy generation below.

# A fast and frugal strategy generation format

While I certainly recommend following the remaining three steps as well, you now have the basic ingredients for strategy generation. If you just want to stick to the basics for now, this can be a productive way to proceed:

1. Get a handful of people together who are quite different and relevant for your strategy. You could also do this on your own, but variety usually helps.
2. Print or draw the Strategy Sketch on a large sheet of paper. At least DIN A3 / Tabloid format, but bigger is better. Put it on a table or wall so that everyone can see it.
3. Map out your current strategy using the first set of 'Questions to ask' for each element. Write down short statements directly on the paper or using sticky notes.
4. Gather new ideas using the other questions, examples, beyond-the-obvious exercises, and inspirational checklists. Write these ideas down too, preferably using another color.
5. Pick the three best ideas and develop them further on a clean Strategy Sketch. Build a complete Strategy Sketch that shows a coherent picture around these ideas. This works particularly well if you take different value propositions or customer groups as a starting point.
6. Go away and test your ideas in practice with customers, suppliers, employees, and others.
7. Come back, evaluate, and repeat until you're done.

# 5

# Assessing strategy

This chapter presents Step 3 of the strategy generation process: Assessing strategy. It presents nine Strategy Checks that can be used to assess your current or new strategy, or to compare strategic options. You don't always need all of them, but together these checks form an extensive assessment toolbox that should give detailed insights into the quality of your strategy. It also includes a short version on page 132 – the Strategy Checklist.

> **Assessing Strategy**
> Judging and testing the quality of the organization's strategy against relevant criteria.

## Why and when to assess your strategy

There is one obvious reason why you want to assess your strategy: To know whether it is good enough. While mapping it, you might already have some idea about the quality of your strategy. You might have encountered inconsistencies, problems, or possible ways to improve it. On top of this, it pays off if you do your assessment in a more systematic way. Therefore, the third step of the strategy generation process is assessing strategy. I am certainly not suggesting you should always do a formal, quantitative, or complex evaluation. However, it is generally a good idea to do a couple of checks to find out whether your strategy fulfills the basic criteria.

# Step 3

There are two logical points where you may want to assess your strategy. The first is *before* you start thinking about new strategy. After you have mapped your strategy in the previous step, assessing it gives you a lot of information about whether it requires improvement and where it can be improved. This is valuable input for the next step – innovating strategy. In some cases, the insights you get might in this way can be so good that you can even skip this whole step: Once you know the problems, the solution might be obvious.

The second point when you want to assess your strategy is *after* you have come up with a new strategy. In this case you do your assessment after step 4 (Innovating strategy). The main reason at this point is that you want to get an idea of the quality of your newly developed strategy. So, before you are going to spend a lot of money and energy on executing it, you want to check whether it is likely going to succeed or not. At this point you might also have generated a number of strategic options or possible directions rather than just one. In that case, assessment helps you choose between these options.

"It is generally a good idea to do a couple of checks to find out whether your strategy fulfills the basic criteria."

## Nine strategy checks

While there is an endless number of criteria that you can use to assess your strategy, I have found the following nine particularly useful.

1 **Coherence check:** Do the elements match? Do they add up to a coherent strategy or not?
2 **Efficiency check:** Are all elements used up to their maximum potential? Can they be better exploited?
3 **Effectiveness check:** Does the strategy work? Are you achieving what you want and getting an adequate performance?
4 **Uniqueness check:** Is the strategy unique enough? Or can it be executed by many other organizations as well?
5 **Flexibility check:** Is the strategy sufficiently flexible? Can it easily be adapted to changes if necessary?

6  **Robustness check:** Can the strategy survive for a sufficiently long time? Is it not too sensitive to changes in the environment?

7  **Scalability check:** Is the strategy scalable? Can it grow easily without too much extra effort and investments?

8  **Responsibility check:** Does the strategy comply with ethical and moral standards? Is it right what is being done?

9  **Pros & cons check:** Do the benefits, advantages, and strengths of the strategy outweigh its costs, disadvantages, and weaknesses?

Each of these strategy checks is further explained in the following pages. You will also find a brief Strategy Checklist on page 132 that helps you to check your strategy in a fast and frugal way.

# 1 Coherence check

Good strategy is coherent and without too many contradictions. Therefore, a first check that you want to do is to assess whether your strategy is sufficiently coherent. This is done by looking at the relationships between the ten elements and assessing whether they make sense in combination. With ten elements, the number of possible combinations is virtually unlimited and it makes no sense to look at all of them. If there are particular combinations that are especially important for your organization, you should definitely look at those. If, on the other hand, you don't have any upfront idea which relationships are most important, I suggest checking the following eleven combinations. These are the ones I find myself regularly referring to in my own work.

A  **Resources & competences + Organizational climate + Values & goals.** *Does what you want and aspire to match with what you actually have or can do with the organization?* To check this you can start with your values and goals and ask whether it is realistic to obtain the required means and organizational climate. You can also start with your means and organizational climate and check whether your values and goals are challenging enough but also not out of reach for your organization.

B  **Resources & competences + Partners.** *Who has the most important resources and competences; you or your partners?* While it is good to have strong partners, your value proposition should not depend more on them than on your own strengths. Also check whether there is not too much overlap between your own resources and competences and theirs.

C **Customers & needs + Value proposition + Competitors.** *Does your value proposition really match what your customers need and is it sufficiently different from what competitors offer?* When customers compare your offer to that of competitors, they should have sufficient reason to choose for you. Therefore you want to check whether you are actually creating the kind of value your customers are looking for.

D **Customers & needs + Value proposition + Values & goals.** *Is what you offer and who you offer it to in line with your values and goals?* There might be a tendency to be opportunistic and to say yes to whatever customer that comes your way – especially in difficult times. But if this dilutes your strategy or keeps you away from what you actually say you want to focus on, it might be better to say no to some customers.

E **Revenue model + Risk & cost management.** *Is your revenue sufficient relative to the risks and costs you bear?* Your strategy can both start with the intention to maximize returns as well as to minimize and control the risks and costs you are willing to bear. Whatever starting point you choose, though, you want to make sure that your risks and costs are not disproportionally high compared to your revenues.

F **Revenue model + Values & goals.** *Which one takes a more important role in your strategy: generating revenue or sticking to your values and goals?* Like with combination E above, you might be tempted to go for the money rather than sticking to what you actually want. This is found to be especially challenging in social businesses, but it applies to any organization. Ideally, you want the two to align with each other.

G **Values & goals + Risks & costs.** *Are the risks and costs associated with your strategy acceptable for the organization?* Any strategy comes with a particular level of risks and costs. Whether these are acceptable depends on the values and goals that are important for the organization. If, for example, trust, reliability, and certainty are key values, you probably want to bear less risks and costs than if entrepreneurship, fast growth, and boldness are emphasized. Therefore, you need to assess whether the risks and costs of your strategy are in line with the organization's values and goals.

**H** **Customers & needs + Partners + Competitors.** *Do your external stakeholders play the role they should play?* Customers, partners, and competitors are the external parties you work for, with, and against. You should keep in mind that these are roles and that a single organization can play multiple roles. Therefore, it is useful to check whether you engage with them in the right role. It might be, for example, that it is more productive to see some of your partners as your customers, and so on.

**I** **Values & goals + Partners.** *Do you work with partners that match you own values and goals?* The best partners are partners that have similar values and goals as you. This facilitates the collaboration, and makes it more likely that you realize your values and goals. Therefore, you want to know whether your partners find the same things important as you or whether there are mismatches that can hinder fruitful cooperation. For the latter you need to decide what to do. Do you adjust your values and goals, stop collaborating, try to reach an agreement, or do you just go on?

**J** **Trends & uncertainties + Values & goals.** *How do you combine seizing opportunities happening in your environment and sticking to your goals?* Seizing opportunities might help you, but it might also lead you to drift away from your goals. When sticking to your values and goals you actually follow your strategy, but you also might miss out on opportunities. Since both have their advantages and disadvantages choices need to be made.

**K** **Trends & uncertainties + Resources & competences + Competitors.** *Are the things happening around you more beneficial or threatening for you or for your competitors?* The trends and uncertainties in your environment might look good or bad for you. However, they might also be good or bad for your competitors. Therefore, you want to know who is better equipped to deal with them.

# 2 Efficiency check

The second check that you can do to assess your strategy is an efficiency check. This check answers the question as to whether you are using the ten elements to their full potential, or whether there is room for improvement. This check applies to all ten elements of the Strategy Sketch:

1. **Resources & competences.** Do you use all your resources and competences and do you use them in the best possible way? Or is there still capacity, information, skills, knowledge, etc. that could be better exploited?

2. **Partners.** Do you have all the partners you need and do you have the best partners you can find? Do you use all the relevant strengths of your partners? Do you benefit at least as much as they do from the partnership?

3. **Customers & needs.** Do you serve the best possible customers and do you serve as many of their needs as you realistically can? Or are there still better customers or needs that you could serve as well?

4. **Competitors.** Do you do all you can to outperform, avoid, or benefit from your competitors? Do you focus on the competitors that are best for you? Do you benefit at least as much from them as they do from you?

5. **Value proposition.** Do you offer the best value proposition that you can offer with your organization? Do you create as much value as you can with your strategy, or are there ways to increase this?

6. **Revenue model.** Do you use all the revenue-generating options there are? Does everyone that benefits from your strategy also sufficiently pay in one way or another? Or can they pay more?

7. **Risk & costs.** Do you minimize the costs and risks you bear, or are there still unnecessary ones that you can avoid?

8. **Values & goals.** Are all the relevant values and goals made explicit and do you really focus on them? Do you use them sufficiently as drivers and motivators for the organization?

9. **Organizational climate.** Do you have the best organizational climate that you can imagine? Does it sufficiently foster the execution of your strategy? Do you use it sufficiently to your advantage?

10. **Trends & uncertainties.** Have you identified the most relevant trends and uncertainties? Do you use them to your advantage in the best possible way?

# 3 Effectiveness check

A third strategy check that you want to do is an effectiveness check. Basically, with this check you assess whether your strategy works or not. Two dimensions of this check are important: What criteria you use (what do you measure?), and what you use as a yardstick (what do you compare your performance to so that you know whether it is good or bad?).

## Effectiveness criteria

With respect to the criteria we can distinguish between a *basic*, overall effectiveness check and a *refined*, element-based effectiveness check. To do a basic effectiveness check you could use the popular 'Triple bottom line' (or 3Ps), which is widely adopted by organizations all over the world. Following this framework, your should assess your strategy in terms of:

- **Profit,** or economic impact. For this criterion numerous financial ratios can be used such as ROI (return on investment), EBITDA (earnings before interest, tax, depreciation, and amortization), or EPS (earnings per share) – to name just a few.
- **People,** or social impact. This concerns the positive and negative impact of the strategy on its employees, communities or other type of stakeholder. Instruments to measure social impact include SROI (social return on investment) and SIA (social impact assessment).
- **Planet,** or ecological impact. This concerns the positive or negative environmental impact of the strategy. The Ecological footprint or Trucost approach are examples of instruments to measure against this criterion.

"You should be quite picky and select only those criteria that you find especially relevant for your organization."

If you don't know all these assessment instruments – which is quite likely since not all of them are widely used yet – you can look them up on the Internet by just typing in their name, or by searching more broadly using terms such as "financial ratios" and "social impact measurement." A useful document to look for is the Catalog of Approaches to Impact Measurement by Olsen and Galimidi.

# Step 3

For a more *refined* effectiveness check you assess each element of the Strategy Sketch separately. While a basic effectiveness check gives you a good impression of the overall effectiveness of your strategy, a refined check provides you with more actionable information. Once you find out that a particular element of the strategy doesn't meet your standards, it is clear that that element needs to be improved. The following criteria can be used for a refined effectiveness check:

| Element | Example criteria |
| --- | --- |
| Resources & competences | Capacity utilization level; Brand value; % of sales spent on R&D; Number of training hours per employee; Number of patents; Projected future earnings; Return on investment. |
| Partners | Number of partners; Partner satisfaction level; Diversity of partners; Number of complaints per partner; Time spent on negations per partner. |
| Customers & needs | Number of customers; Customer satisfaction level; Customer loyalty; Order quantity; Number of repeat orders; Profitability per customer; Number of new customers through customers. |
| Competitors | Number of competitors; Market share; Growth rate of the market; Concentration ratio; Average margin in the industry; Herfindahl index; Number of new competitors. |
| Value proposition | Design, usefulness, quality, and reliability of product/service; Punctuality of delivery; Value-for-money. |
| Revenue model | Sales revenues; Discounted cash flow; EBITDA; Profitability per product; Earnings per share; Growth rate. |
| Risk & costs | Number of defects, delays, and injuries; Potential loss x probably of risk; Annual loss expectancy; Liquidity; Solvency; Fixed/variable costs; Inventory conversion period. |

| Values & goals | Clarity of values and goals; Awareness level; Compliance with legal and ethical standards; Clarity of performance indicators; Degree of monitoring and control against values and goals. |
|---|---|
| Organiza-tional climate | Employee satisfaction; Employee turnover; Absenteeism rate; Degree of formalization; Degree of employee initiative; Openness of communication; Risk tolerance. |

For the final element (Trends & uncertainties) there are no real effectiveness criteria since it refers to the context within which you operate. Yet, overall the balance should be that the context should be beneficial for you. If not, you should consider moving elsewhere or to adopt a strategy that benefits more from the context.

Together, these nine types of effectiveness criteria form quite a comprehensive measurement system for measuring how effective your strategy is. Compared to the currently most-used approach – the Balanced Scorecard – this set of criteria is much richer and therefore more complete. Generally, this is an advantage, because it allows you to develop more detailed and relevant insights into the strategic performance of your organization. However, you should make sure that you don't use all of them. This will be way too much and it will complicate your strategy process or even let it stagnate. Therefore, you should be quite picky and select only those criteria that you find especially relevant for your organization. A handful or two should be enough.

## Yardsticks

Assessing your strategy against these criteria gives you a lot of information about the effectiveness of your strategy. However, to judge whether your scores are good or bad, you also need to compare them to some sort of standard – so you need a yardstick. There are three types of yardstick you can think of:

- **Goal-based yardstick:** First, you can use your own goals as a main yardstick for assessing your strategy against the criteria above. The main question then is whether or not you achieve what you want with these various criteria. If, for example, your aim was to achieve a revenue increase of 10%, you can measure your performance against this aim.

- **Relative yardstick:** You can also compare yourself to others and thus take a relative point of comparison. Think, for example, of an industry average, or a comparison with your most important competitors. Along those lines you can assess, for example, whether your employee turnover is below, on, or above your industry's average.
- **Absolute yardstick:** Finally, for some criteria there are commonly adopted threshold values that can be used as a yardstick. Examples are the 'quick ratio' which generally should be 1 or higher; or 'zero waste' – which should be zero.

# 4 Uniqueness check

As the definition of strategy indicates, good strategy aims at developing a unique and sustainable way of value creation. Accordingly, a fourth criterion against which you want to assess your strategy is its uniqueness. Three aspects of uniqueness are important: The sources of uniqueness, the degree of uniqueness, and the sustainability of uniqueness.

## Sources of uniqueness

Strategies can be unique in many ways. In fact, uniqueness can be found in all but two of the ten elements of the Strategy Sketch. The two exceptions are competitors since those are the ones you compare yourself to and trends and uncertainties since these reflect the environment, which is also relevant for competitors. So, to assess the uniqueness of your strategy, you can compare your strategy to that of competitors and judge whether you...

- ...possess unique resources or competences that others don't have.
- ...have access to unique partners in your network.
- ...offer one or more unique value propositions.
- ...have access to a unique group of customers.
- ...use a unique revenue model, a way of making money.
- ...have a unique risk or cost advantage or way of managing these.
- ...have unique values or goals that drive the organization.
- ...have a unique organizational culture or structure.

If one or more of these elements is indeed unique, this is a good basis for building your strategy. This applies even if this uniqueness may look bad initially (such as high fixed costs, a negative organizational climate, or customers that systematically complain and pay late).

Although perhaps bad in your current strategy, they reflect what you currently have. Try seeing them as strengths and find a way to use them. You might, for example, have costs that are relatively high but also largely variable, have employees that complain because they care, or have customers that want to tell you something through their annoying behavior. Of course, not all uniquely 'bad' characteristics can be turned into advantages. However, it is still useful to at least have a look at them in this way.

## Degrees of uniqueness

Your strategy need not be 100% unique. That would be impossible and even if it were feasible you would have such an obscure organization that it would be very unlikely that it would attract many customers. On the other hand, your strategy is never completely identical to your competitors' strategy, if only because your organization's name, people, location, or customers are different. In between these extremes, it makes a lot of sense to assess the degree to which your strategy is unique. When you do this, it is useful to identify which of the following five degrees of uniqueness apply to your strategy:

1. **Unique to the organization.** Your strategy is new for you but is already used by your competitors. This is usually not so good since it means you are not unique anymore.

2. **Unique to the region.** Your strategy is similar to strategies used in other regions (another continent, country, city, and so on) but is not used yet in your region.
   *Example:* Ryanair's low-cost strategy, which was already used by South-West Airlines in the United States.

3. **Unique to the market segment.** Your strategy has been used to serving particular groups of customers, but not the ones you are addressing.
   *Example:* Car manufacturers offering features for cars in the lower segments which were previously only available to higher segments.

4. **Unique to the industry.** Your strategy looks like strategies used in other industries, but has not been used in your industry so far.
   *Example:* Airbnb's home-sharing strategy which looks like car-sharing strategies.

5. **Unique to the world.** As far as you know, no one else has done something similar to you. This can be really good and groundbreaking but also risky.
   *Example:* Cirque du Soleil's unique combination of theatre and circus.

*Increasing level of uniqueness*

123

Generally, the more unique your strategy is, the more potential it has. However, the risks increase too, so you always should assess whether the level of uniqueness is suitable for you.

## "It is nice to be unique today, but what if others see what you do and copy it as soon as they can?"

### Sustainability of uniqueness

A third aspect of uniqueness that you need in order to assess your strategy is the sustainability of that uniqueness. It is nice to be unique today, but what if others see what you do and copy it as soon as they can? Where does that leave you with all your efforts? To assess the sustainability of your uniqueness, you can ask the following five questions:

A. Can (parts of) your strategy be legally protected by patents, copyrights, trademarks, or other legal forms?
*Example:* LEGO's (expired) patent on their blocks.

B. Can (parts of) your strategy be monopolized so that you are the only one able to use it?
*Example:* Relying on resources that are extremely rare.

C. Can (parts of) your strategy be kept secret or hidden for competitors so that they don't know enough to copy?
*Example:* DuPont's trade secret for producing Kevlar.

D. Can (parts of) your strategy be made so complex that they are virtually impossible to understand by others?
*Example:* Relying on tacit knowledge and experience.

E. Can (parts of) your strategy be made so difficult to copy that competitors give up before they try?
*Example:* Relying on a large network of partners.

If you want your strategy to be sustainable and imitation-proof, the answer to at least one of these questions should be yes. If this is not the case, these five questions show you the various ways in which you could make it harder to imitate.

# 5 Flexibility check

Given that change happens everywhere, you also want your strategy to be sufficiently flexible so that you can quickly respond, innovate, and adjust. Of course a strategy should not be changed all the time, but not being *able* to change it when necessary is a problem that you want to avoid. As with the previous checks, this strategy check is also relevant for all the elements of your strategy. Therefore, to assess the flexibility of your strategy, you should ask the following questions:

1. **Resources & competences:** Are you able to keep your resources and competences up to date? Do you renew them enough? Can you get rid of them if necessary?
2. **Partners:** Can you switch to other partners if necessary? Are you not too dependent on some of them? Can you easily get new partners or let existing partners go?
3. **Customers & needs:** Are you sufficiently aware of the changing needs or habits of your customers? Can you quickly adjust your offer to new customers or to new customer needs?
4. **Competitors:** Are you sufficiently aware of your competitors and their strategies? Can you respond quickly enough to their actions?
5. **Value proposition:** Can you improve or change your products or services easily? Can you offer new or additional products or services if required?
6. **Revenue model:** Can you easily change the way you make money? Can you increase prices without losing too many customers?
7. **Risk & costs:** Can you easily change your risk profile? Can you change your cost structure when circumstances ask for it?
8. **Values & goals:** Are your goals and plans sufficiently flexible? Do you change them enough when circumstances ask for it?
9. **Organizational climate:** Is the culture or structure of your organization sufficiently flexible? Are people able to change their habits, jobs, or ways of working?
10. **Trends & uncertainties:** Are you sufficiently sensitive to changes in your environment? Can you respond quickly enough to the trends and uncertainties that you face?

Not all the elements of your strategy should necessarily be flexible. If they are, there is a great chance that your organization will drift and lack a clear and recognizable profile. Furthermore, there are no clear rules that tell you how flexible you need to be. That depends very much on the dynamics and complexity of your industry and on whether your strategy is built around being flexible or not. This means that it is largely up to your own judgment whether you think your strategy is sufficiently flexible or not. You do want to make sure, though, that none of the elements of your strategy really lock you in and form a barrier against change and innovation.

> "Compared to a flexible strategy, a robust strategy has the advantage that it gives the organization stability."

# 6 Robustness check

Ensuring that your strategy is flexible is one way of dealing with changes. Another way is to make your strategy more robust. A robust strategy is a strategy that, as a whole, can remain largely unchanged even when there are changes in some of its elements or in the environment. Compared to a flexible strategy, a robust strategy has the advantage that it gives the organization stability, rather than that it requires continuous adaptations.

The most comprehensive way of assessing the robustness of your strategy is to come up with a number of scenarios and judge whether your strategy is capable of dealing with the majority of them. If this is indeed the case, it indicates that your strategy is not affected by changes in your environment – and is therefore robust. This gives you some degree of certainty that your strategy holds true, even if things might turn out differently than you expected. On page 100, I briefly discussed the steps of scenario planning. To carry out this strategy check, I suggest you follow these steps to develop various scenarios and then to assess to what extent your strategy holds true in those different scenarios.

Another way to assess the robustness of your strategy is to ask yourself what happens to the other elements if one element of your strategy changes significantly. Thus, for example, if your most important people were to leave the organization (reflecting a change in resources and competences), could you still offer the same value proposition to the same customers? Or, if your biggest customer suddenly left, would your revenue model still be profitable? To put it a bit more systematically, you can ask the following three questions for each element of the Strategy Sketch:

- If something *disappears* in this element, can the other elements and the strategy as a whole remain unchanged?
- If something is *added* to this element, can the other elements and the strategy as a whole remain unchanged?
- If something *changes* in this element, can the other elements and the strategy as a whole remain unchanged?

# 7 Scalability check

As a seventh check you may also want to assess whether your strategy is scalable enough. A scalable strategy is a strategy that is suitable for growth. This means that you can increase your revenue or impact relatively easily compared to the extra effort this would require and that there are no substantial barriers against growth. Scalability seems unimportant for some organizations. After all, if you don't want to grow, you probably don't care too much about scalability. However, even then it might still be useful to assess your strategy's scalability. This will show you whether you could achieve the same revenue or impact with less effort. And who doesn't want that? There can be growth barriers related to each of the ten elements of the Strategy Sketch. To identify them, you can use the following questions: In case you want to grow substantially...

1. **Resources & competences:** Are their enough resources available? Can you get the people you need? Do you have the capacity and skills to produce on a larger scale?
2. **Partners:** Can you get sufficient and suitable suppliers? Can they deliver everything you would need?
3. **Customers & needs:** Are there enough potential customers? Is the overall market large enough?
4. **Competitors:** Doesn't the competition increase too much? Would your growth not occur at the expense of your competitors?
5. **Value proposition:** Do your products and services appeal to a large market? Are they not limited to a particular niche?

6. **Revenue model:** Would the revenue model still work if sales increased substantially? What about the pricing strategy?

7. **Risk & costs:** Would your risks and costs rise less than your revenue? Or at least not more than your revenue?

8. **Values & goals:** Do people in the organization want to grow? Is growth in line with the organization's values and goals?

9. **Organizational climate:** Is the organizational structure suitable for growth? What about the organizational culture?

10. **Trends & uncertainties:** Are you still able to respond to ongoing trends? Are you facing important new uncertainties?

The more affirmative answers you can give to these questions, the better the scalability of your strategy. If you want a more refined scalability check than a simple yes/no answer, you can use the following classifications to assess each element:

- **Green:** Doesn't need adjustment. It's already scalable, so the current strategy is no problem for growth.
- **Amber:** Can be adjusted but requires some attention. Can be made scalable and growth is possible with some extra effort.
- **Red:** Impossible to adjust. Serious scalability barrier. Requires substantial reorientation of the strategy.

# 8 Responsibility check

Good strategy is not only good in terms of benefits for the organization, but also in terms of societal norms and values. Views on what is good, though, can differ quite radically:

A. On the one extreme there is the 'shareholder view.' This argues that it is good for the organization and for society if the organization aims exclusively at generating revenue for its shareholders. The reason is that organizations will try to make the best of their resources in this way. And if everyone does this, society as a whole is better off. Thus, in this view a strategy is good if it maximizes shareholder value.

(B) On the other extreme there is the 'stakeholder view.' This argues the other way around: It is good for the organization and its stakeholders if the organization is good for other stakeholders as well. The reason is that organizations depend on their stakeholders. Only by satisfying them can the organization sustain its position over time. Thus, from this point of view strategy should do well for others too.

In practice, you probably combine these two views. Often the interest of the organization itself takes priority over the interests of others, although others are taken into account too.

In this eighth strategy check, you assess whether the strategy takes the interests of various stakeholders sufficiently into account. There are two versions of this check: A simple one and an elaborate one.

## A simple responsibility check

For a simple approach to assess whether your strategy is responsible or not, you can use Texas Instruments' guidelines for ethical decision-making, as referred to on page 92. It consists of the following six questions:

- Is everything that needs to be done to realize the strategy legal? If not, change it.
- Does your strategy comply with organizational and societal values? If not, change it.
- Does your strategy require you to do anything that would make you feel bad? If so, change it.
- How would it look if newspapers reported about your strategy? Bad? Change it.
- Do you know whether the things you need to do to realize your strategy are right or wrong? If yes, change it.
- You aren't sure? Ask until you get an answer.

## A more elaborate responsibility check

If you want to know more specifically whether your strategy is responsible and whether it makes the organization do the right thing, you can carry out a more elaborate responsibility check. This check includes two sets of questions. The first is about whether you sufficiently avoid causing negative effects and the second about whether you sufficiently generate positive effects.

# Step 3

| Questions for assessing whether you sufficiently *avoid negative* effects: | Questions for assessing whether you sufficiently *generate positive* effects: |
|---|---|
| • Are any people mistreated? Think of employees, suppliers, customers, neighbors, communities, etc. | • Do you make peoples' lives better? Think of employees, suppliers, customers, neighbors, communities, etc. |
| • Are any resources depleted? Think specifically about natural resources with limited availability. | • Do you create or upgrade resources so that they can be used in a better way? Think of the treatment of materials or energy as byproduct. |
| • Is there any waste or pollution that could be avoided? Think of energy and unrecyclable materials. | • Do you add something valuable to the world? Is it better off with your organization than without? |
| • Do you use or get more than you actually need? Think of revenue, luxuries, bonuses, etc. | • Do you let others benefit from what you don't really need? Think about philanthropy, charities, etc. |
| • Do you create or increase social problems? Think of reduced standards of living or wellbeing, inequality, injustice, reduced freedom, etc. | • Do you solve or reduce social problems? Think of improving the standard of living, wellbeing, equality, justice, freedom, etc. |
| • Do you, intentionally or unintentionally, encourage others to make a negative impact? Think about setting a bad example, promoting unethical behavior, etc. | • Do you, intentionally or unintentionally, stimulate others to make a positive contribution to the world? Think about lecturing, foundations, role model, etc. |

The more affirmative answers you have in the left column, the more room there is for improvement. And the more affirmative answers you have in the right column, the more your strategy is responsible.

# 9 Pros & cons check

The last check you want to carry out is a comparison of the pros (benefits, advantages, strengths) of the strategy with its cons (costs, disadvantages, weaknesses). No strategy will completely fulfill all the eight other criteria and every strategy has its downsides and weak points as well. Therefore, the point of doing all these assessments is not to arrive at some perfect utopian strategy. Looking for that will paralyze you rather than help you move on. No, what you want is a strategy where the pros substantially outweigh the cons. Therefore it makes sense to compare them. As with the responsibility check, there are two versions of this check: A simple one and an elaborate one.

## A simple pros & cons check

The simplest way to do this check is to make a list of all the pros and cons of the strategy that you can come up with. So, start listing all the positives aspects of the strategy such as its benefits, advantages, and strengths. Then move on to the negative aspects including the costs, disadvantages, and weaknesses. After listing both you can make a judgment as to whether overall the pros outweigh the cons.

If you are with a group, you could also divide the group in two. Let one half of the group be the promoters and ask them to list all the pros of the strategy and defend it. The other half of the group are the protesters, so ask them to list all the cons and to attack the strategy. After this you compare the arguments for and against the strategy and judge its quality.

## A more elaborate pros & cons check

A more elaborate way of doing a pros & cons check is by using the eight previous criteria as a framework. Instead of just listing the pros and cons of the strategy, do this for each of the eight criteria. So, with respect to coherence, list the strong points of the strategy and its weak points. Do the same for efficiency, effectiveness, and so on.

As an alternative elaborate pros & con check, you can also use the ten elements of the Strategy Sketch. In that case, list the pros and cons for each element separately.

"The point of doing all these assessments is not to arrive at some perfect utopian strategy. Looking for that will paralyze you rather than help you move on."

## A quick strategy checklist

Doing all nine strategy checks in a comprehensive manner will cost you a lot of time and effort. Sometimes this is necessary, especially if you want to be as sure as possible that your strategy fulfills the most important requirements. However, in case you want a quick insight, you can also use the checklist below. It covers every check with a single question.

| | Yes | Maybe | No |
|---|---|---|---|
| **Coherence check** <br> Do all the elements of your strategy fit together? | ○ | ○ | ○ |
| **Efficiency check** <br> Do you use everything you have to its full potential? | ○ | ○ | ○ |
| **Effectiveness check** <br> Does your strategy do what it is supposed to do? | ○ | ○ | ○ |
| **Uniqueness check** <br> Is your strategy sufficiently different from others? | ○ | ○ | ○ |
| **Flexibility check** <br> Can you change your strategy easily enough? | ○ | ○ | ○ |

| | Yes | Maybe | No |
|---|---|---|---|
| **Robustness check** <br> Can you maintain your strategy when things are changing around you? | ○ | ○ | ○ |
| **Scalability check** <br> Can you grow without too much extra effort? | ○ | ○ | ○ |
| **Responsibility check** <br> Are you doing the right thing? | ○ | ○ | ○ |
| **Pros & cons check** <br> Do the pros of the strategy outweigh its cons? | ○ | ○ | ○ |

# How to use the strategy checks

As I pointed out at the beginning of this chapter, there are two points at which assessment is important: a) An assessment of your *current* strategy as a starting point for innovating it, and b) an assessment of your *newly generated* strategy to get a sense of its quality before you actually execute it. In the second case, you might also have developed several strategic options between which you want to choose. In that case, you can use the strategy checks to assess which of the options is preferable.

At whatever point you do the assessment, the nine strategy checks can be used in various ways. You can use them, for example, quickly as a checklist in the back of your mind, but you can also turn them into a formal assessment that requires extensive information gathering and analysis. Roughly you have the following options:

**Use them as informal checklist.** After having read this chapter you will have a sense of what kind of criteria are important to judge strategy. While moving through the strategy generation process, you can use this knowledge informally or implicitly when you think about whether your (existing or new) strategy is good enough. If you're with a team, you could judge the strategy or the different strategic options that you have generated during an informal conversation.

**Peer review.** To overcome personal bias or groupthink and to avoid missing important gaps or opportunities, it is recommended to have others in the organization look at the strategy too. You can, for example, ask a group of employees to critically assess the strategy that you have come up with, thereby using some or all of the strategy checks. An additional advantage of involving them at this stage is that they might easier commit to the strategy once it has crystalized further.

**Customer and supplier testing.** Another useful way to assess your strategy is to test it with customers and/or important partners such as suppliers. In the end, customers are the ones who buy your products or services, so their opinions matter very much. Along the same lines, suppliers are also needed to realize the strategy and they might have very good insights that you lack. You probably don't want to use all the strategy checks with them, but for the uniqueness check in particular they are important.

**Formal assessment and valuation.** A fourth way to assess your strategy is a formal assessment whereby you systematically evaluate the strategy against the criteria of the nine strategy checks. This type of assessment typically requires you to quantify the criteria and to gather as objective data as possible to make sure your conclusions are right. Making an extensive business case is also an example of this type of assessment.

"Formal and extensive assessment might help more to reduce perceived uncertainty, than that it reduces actual uncertainty."

While all four options can work in practice, their order and priority is in most cases as presented above. The first option is the very least that you should always do. You want to keep at least some of the criteria in the back of your mind while you go through the strategy generation process. Strategy is too important to let personal bias or groupthink play a crucial role.

There is nothing principally against formal and extensive assess-ments, and especially in cases where substantial investments have to be made, these might be extremely valuable. Generally though, this type of assessment tends to be overused. It costs a lot of time, effort, and money and it might help more to reduce one's *perceived* uncertainty, than that it reduces *actual* uncertainty. In other words, you might feel better after a formal assessment, but the actual added value of the information gathered can be questionable. This is especially the case in markets that are very uncertain, such as very new, complex, or dynamic markets. In these kinds of markets, the available information might simply be irrelevant. Therefore, the best way to assess your strategy there is to go out and test it for real with customers, suppliers, or other stakeholders.

## In case you need to prioritize

After carrying out the various checks listed above you might have found many points for improvement for your strategy. It is unlikely, though, that you can address all of them at the same time. Therefore, before moving on to the next step, it can be useful to prioritize the issues that you found and focus your energy on the most important ones.

A simple way to do this is to look at all nine checks and list the ones where you scored a 'no' in the Strategy Checklist, or where you found substantial issues. Then you ask yourself which of these issues is the biggest obstacle for making progress, or which of the issues is most urgent and important. Is it the fact that your strategy is incoherent, or that it is inefficient, or that it is ineffective? And so on. Picking the key issue in this way gives you a starting point as to where and how you should innovate your strategy at the next step of the strategy generation process.

# The**four**examples

## Strategy assessment at Macman

Macman's main strategic challenge as they see it themselves is that they cannot come up with the next 'big idea' that can replace their reliance on steel cutting and bending machines. While that is important, the strategy assessment reveals two additional issues:

1. **Not flexible.** Macman is strongly invested in their technology. Their resources and competences are fully dedicated to producing steel cutting and bending machines. Furthermore, they rely on two large customers, giving them very little room for maneuver.
2. **Not efficient.** This is rather obvious from the 20% of unused capacity they report. More importantly, perhaps, is that they only serve a small part of their customers' needs. Next to cutting and bending machines they need transportation belts, grinders, drilling machines, and so on. As the customers would prefer to buy these from Macman, there is an unmet demand.

## Strategy assessment at Hospicare

The assessment of Hospicare's current strategy reveals two main bottlenecks:

1. **Not effective.** Although proud of their performance, they are actually only effective in one indicator: The percentage of successful operations. They do not do so well on other indicators. Patients, for example, are dissatisfied and want more 'humane' treatment, and the personnel don't like the businesslike climate of the hospital.
2. **Not coherent.** Hospicare's ambition to go partly commercial might not fit in with their current poor customer orientation. Currently, patients don't have much choice, but if they were to turn into real customers, they would have to put their customers/patients first and listen to their actual needs.

## Strategy assessment at GoforIT

Things are going well at GoforIT, although the assessment shows up two issues that require attention:

1 **Not unique.** GoforIT's products are unique. However, their competences aren't. As they acknowledge themselves, their software is rather easy to copy, and they outsource almost everything they do. This makes their strategy very vulnerable in the medium to long-term.

2 **Not responsible.** GoforIT does very well for its two founders. They have made an incredible amount of money in a few years, but so far no one else has really benefitted. They don't pay their suppliers well and their 19 employees hardly profit from the firm's financial success. GoforIT could do much more to make a positive impact.

The efficiency check shows furthermore that GoforIT is not efficient at all. Their technology is not yet fully used, and their market is far from saturated. Given the state of development of the company, though, this lack of efficiency is not an issue – it means there is still plenty of potential for further growth.

## Strategy assessment at Comcom

Being a one-person company, the assessment of Comcom's strategy is not very complicated. A quick scan with the strategy checklist confirms what Anisha already knew: Her strategy is not unique and not scalable. She doesn't do anything unique compared to her competitors and her reliance on hourly rates makes she cannot increase her income without working more.

# Innovating strategy

This chapter explains Step 4 of the strategy generation process: Innovating strategy. It is during this step that new strategy is actually generated. It presents five different approaches to strategic innovation. As the suitability of these approaches depends on the amount of freedom you have in generating new strategy, I start with a brief discussion on that.

> *Innovating strategy:*
> **Renewing and redesigning the organization's strategy through incremental or radical innovation.**

## Defining your latitude for strategic innovation

Strategic innovation is rarely completely unbounded. How many organizations are willing and capable of completely letting their existing business go and doing something completely new? Not so many, and usually that is a good thing. Whether you are involved in a startup or a large mature organization, there are nearly always things that you have built up in the past and that can be a good basis for new strategy. Think about all the knowledge, experience, and contacts you have. These are probably useful to rely on in your new strategy as well. This means strategy generation is just as much about changing and improving your existing strategy and about letting things go than about generating entirely new strategy (see also the section on 'Strategy generation is emergent' on page 29).

139

# Step 4

Also, you might face explicit restrictions that cause you to not have complete freedom in redesigning your strategy. Maybe you are part of a bigger organization, or you have clear guidelines, instructions, or regulations that you have to adhere to and which limit your freedom of innovation. Or maybe you already have a clear idea yourself in which direction you want to go, or what the innovation 'task' should be that you want people to work on. When you start innovating your strategy, you want to take these boundaries into account.

> "Once you have specified these boundaries, it is useful to write them down in an explicit strategic innovation task."

On the other hand, strategic innovation would not be strategic innovation if you were to completely stick to business as usual or if you let yourself be too restricted. There is always something in your existing business that you could or should let go, add, or change. And even if there are clear restrictions, or if you might already think you know in which direction the new strategy should go, it can still be useful to look further afield. You might be biased, or think too narrowly, and the restrictions that you see might be less strict than you think (see also the fifth activation tactic in Chapter 3, 'Just start' on page 56). It would be too bad if you missed out on promising opportunities just because the innovation step started out being too narrow-minded.

All of this means that, before you start innovating, it is useful to have a good sense of your 'latitude for innovation' – the freedom that you have to innovate and the boundaries that limit this freedom. The following three types of boundaries are helpful in judging this: Your allowance, your ability, and your willingness to innovate.

### Allowance to innovate: What are you allowed to do?
A first boundary defining your latitude for strategic innovation comes about through what you are allowed to change. You can think of the following boundaries:

- **Legal regulations and social norms and values** that define what you are allowed to do by law and what society finds acceptable.

While these mainly apply to what you currently do, it is quite likely that they also affect how innovative you can be in changing your strategy.

- **Industry standards and habits** that tell you the 'rules of the game.' When you ignore these, you risk becoming too much of an outsider that others don't understand anymore. On the other hand, changing the rules of the game or trying to create a whole new game can be a very fruitful strategy too – this is the key idea of Blue ocean strategy.
- **Policies and financial objectives** by corporate headquarters, the board of directors, or shareholders that tell you what decisions you are allowed to make and what financial objectives should be realized. You might be restricted as to what you can change and what you can't. However, as suggested previously, I wouldn't be too obedient here and try to find out how far you can go.

## Ability to innovate: What are you able to do?

Before you start thinking about your new strategy, you should also take the capabilities of the organization into account. Maybe you are allowed to do something radically different, but are you also able to do it? I am not saying strategy generation should be completely restricted by what is realistic. That will kill most creativity in the process and almost guarantee that you won't come up with any bright ideas. However, you do want some sense of realism and to make sure that you will actually be able to execute the strategy that is being generated. Therefore, it is useful to think of the following boundaries here:

- **Scope:** Does the innovation sufficiently fit your resources and competences? Can you actually do it? You can come up with the wildest ideas for a new strategy, and let's assume they are great and that there is indeed a market for them. But is your organization best equipped to realize these ideas, or are others much more capable of doing it?
- **Capacity:** Do you have the time, people, and money needed to realize your innovation? You don't need to fully specify this upfront, but some sense of your capacity is useful. Otherwise you might generate great new ideas which simply cannot be realized because the capacity is lacking – think especially about the fact that the normal business will probably have to continue while you are busy with your new strategy.
- **Power:** Do you have the power and influence to make the innovation happen? Are you or your organization in the position to

make the required changes or are you dependent on factors that are outside your sphere of influence? If you don't have sufficient power or influence, this doesn't necessarily mean you won't be able to realize your strategy, although it probably means that you need to include others that do have the necessary power or influence.

### Willingness to innovate: What are you willing to do?

A third type of boundary for strategic innovation stems from your own intentions and wishes and those of others in the organization. Maybe you are allowed and able to make a particular strategic innovation, but are you also willing to make it, and does it match the aspirations that you have for the strategy generation process? The following three aspects are relevant here:

- **Readiness:** Are you or others in the organization sufficiently willing to make the required changes? Are people convinced that it is a good thing to do? Are you willing to make the required investments? If not, there is a good chance the strategy you come up with won't be properly executed.
- **Preservation:** Are there things in your strategy that you definitely want to preserve? In answering this question it is useful to go systematically through all the elements of the Strategy Sketch. What do you want to keep and what do you want to let go or change?
- **Aspirations:** What do you want to achieve with the new strategy? Maybe there is just the general aspiration that the organization should perform better or survive. However, there might also be more specific aspirations that give a clear direction as to where the strategy generation process should be heading.

> "Since strategy generation is a creative process with unpredictable outcomes you want to engage it openly."

Most of these boundaries are not written in stone and between the three categories the latter ones are less restrictive than the first. However, they are relevant enough to seriously take into account when to innovate your strategy.

## Writing down the strategic innovation task

Once you have specified the boundaries, it is useful to write them down in an explicit *strategic innovation task*. This will help you make sure that the strategy generation process remains focused and will produce not just wild ideas, but also ideas that are relevant for the organization. You should specify at least the following:

- **Why?** What do you want to achieve through innovating your strategy? Should it lead, for example, to more profits, growth, focus, or scope, or is there a particular problem that should be solved? Also, take into account the outcomes of the assessment step above.
- **When?** What is the timeline, and when should what be ready? Is there, for example, a particular date before which there should be a clear idea, a proof of concept, or a working strategy?
- **Where?** Which part of the organization is involved? Does it concern the whole organization, or a specific business unit, department, or location?

Of course you can specify much more, such as who exactly should be involved at which stage, and how much time and money can be invested. Also, you can make a comprehensive project plan indicating when certain deliverables and milestones should be ready. If possible, though, I would avoid this since it might restrict the strategy generation process too much. Since strategy generation is a creative process with unpredictable outcomes you want to engage it openly. Once things start to crystalize a bit you can start planning more carefully.

The strategic innovation task

What are you allowed to do?

What are you willing to do?

The TASK:
Why, When and Where
to innovate your strategy?

What are you able to do?

# Five strategic innovation approaches

You now have everything it takes to get started with innovating your strategy. Your key stakeholders are activated, you know your current strategy and its strengths and weaknesses, and you have defined your latitude for innovation. This means you can now pick one of the following five innovation approaches and use it:

## 1 Elementary innovation

This approach aims for innovations within one or a few of the ten elements of the Strategy Sketch. For example, you are mainly interested in finding a new group of customers, or a new revenue model. As it leaves much of your strategy untouched, this approach is the least radical type of innovation.

## 2 Amplifying innovation

More radical than the first approach, you can also deliberately aim at innovations that make your strategy more scalable. With this approach you stick mostly to the strategy that you already have, but you aim at expanding it to a larger scale so that your impact or revenue increase.

## 3 Routed innovation

Also more radical than the first, with this approach you take one or two elements of your strategy as a starting point and from there on innovate or even redefine the rest of your strategy. So, you start for example with your means (resources and competences and partners) and from there on innovate the rest. As we will see in this chapter, there are six innovation routes that you could follow.

## 4 Projective innovation

Even more radical than the previous approaches, with this approach you take possible future scenarios as a starting point and from thereon imagine what kind of strategy would fit those scenarios. So, you start by projecting what the world might look like in five, ten, or even twenty years and then generate strategy that would be appropriate in that world.

5 **Freestyle innovation**
   With this most radical type of innovation, you let go of all boundaries
   and go wild. Obviously a reality check is needed at some point, but
   your aim is to start as openly as possible and build attractive castles in
   the air. Thus, with this approach you are really aiming for generating
   strategy that is new for your organization or even new to the world.

   Of course, you don't have to stick to just one approach. You can also
   use them together, or one after another.

## Innovation approach I: Elementary innovation

I don't need to say very much about this first approach of strategic
innovation. As mentioned above, this approach focuses on
innovations within one or few of the elements of the Strategy Sketch.
Thus, for example, you look at your customers and needs and try
to find a new group of customers you can serve, or focus on how
you can adjust your value proposition, or how you can improve your
resources or competences.

In most cases a change in one element of your strategy will also mean
some changes in other elements. If you focus on a new group of
customers, for example, this most likely also implies some adjustments
to your value proposition and to the competitors you are dealing with.
Yet, since this approach aims at making small innovations, the overall
impact on your strategy usually remains modest. For this reason this
approach is mostly of an incremental nature.

Chapter 4 on mapping strategy already contained all the information
and tools needed to use this first approach. Next to the information
helping you to map out your current strategy, the chapter also
included information for elementary innovation – the questions to
ask, the beyond-the-obvious exercises, the inspirational checklists,
the useful models, and the four examples. Based on that information,
elementary innovation can be done by using:

1. The right columns of the 'Questions to ask' tables for each element. While the left column concerns questions about your current strategy, the right column deliberately aims at fostering elementary innovation. Asking yourself these questions can help you think in new directions.

2. The 'Beyond-the-obvious exercises.' While primarily aimed at providing you with more in-depth insights into your current strategy, these exercises can also provide you with new ideas for each of the ten elements of your strategy.

3. The 'Inspirational checklists' that stimulate thinking in new directions by giving examples of what the various elements could look like.

4. The 'Useful models' that help to better understand each element in a systematic manner. They foster the systematic mapping of your current strategy and the generation of new strategy for each of element.

5. The 'Four examples' of Strategy Sketches, which can be used as sources of inspiration for thinking concretely about your new strategy.

## Innovation approach 2: Amplifying innovation

Amplifying innovation is particularly relevant if you want or need to grow substantially in the near future. In Chapter 5 (Assessing strategy) you already saw a scalability check to assess whether a strategy is sufficiently scalable or not. If the conclusion there is that it is not scalable enough, amplifying innovation is the type of innovation you are looking for. This section provides you with a variety of scalability tactics that you can use to do this.

While no black-and-white distinction can be made, product and service organizations generally differ substantially in their scalability. The most important reason is that service-based organizations usually rely more on people's personal skills and time than product-based organizations. This often means that service-based organizations are harder to scale and that one has to look for other scalability tactics than for product-based organizations. Along these lines, we can distinguish between two sets of scalability tactics – one for product-based organizations and one for service-based organizations. While your organization might be primarily oriented towards one of the two, I certainly suggest having a look at both sets.

## Product-based scalability tactics

Various tactics can be used to scale a product-based strategy so that it generates more revenue or impact without a proportional increase in risks or costs. When thinking about your strategy, consider whether you can:

- Improve capacity utilization (like Amazon, exploiting its server capacity outside its peak hours around Thanksgiving).
- Use economies of scale (like Ford in the early days, which drastically reduced its price per car through a combination of automation and increasing the production volume).
- Use network externalities (like Whatsapp, where each new customer adds value to the product at no cost).
- Simplify and standardize the product (like IKEA, which uses a modular design in the vast majority of its products).
- Leverage your core competencies (like Yamaha, which applies its refined metal processing skills to engines, musical instruments, and audio equipment).
- Let others do the work (like Apple, which outsources most of its production to other companies).
- 'Servicefy' your product (like Dropbox, which sells its software and server space as a service).
- Create 'lock in' or 'switching costs,' thus making it harder for customers to switch (like supermarkets or other organizations using customer loyalty cards).

Please note that quite a few of these tactics can be used by service-based organizations as well.

## Service-based scalability tactics

There are also various scalability tactics for service-based strategies. When innovating your strategy, consider whether you can:

- Leverage the skills of seniors to juniors (like hospitals or consultancy firms which let juniors perform the simpler tasks while offering services at senior quality level – and price).
- Materialize your service (like me, or other strategy researchers or consultants who write a book or develop a tool).
- Productize your service (like accountancy firms who charge a fixed price for a predefined service instead of flexible hourly rates).

- Make the service uniform (like McDonalds, which has totally standardized its processes and restaurants).
- Simplify the service to what customers want (like Basic-Fit which strips down gym facilities to the essentials).
- Up-sell to let existing customers buy more (like airlines offering you to upgrade to a better seat).
- Cross-sell between customer groups (like airlines collaborating with car-rental companies and hotel chains allowing the customers of one also buy from the other).
- Automate parts of the service (like banks offering online banking which can be scaled without significant additional costs).
- Make it mobile (like virtual help desks using chat, Facebook, or other non-personal ways of interaction).

You should also note here that quite a few of these tactics can be used by product-based organizations as well.

## Innovation approach 3: Routed innovation

A third approach to innovate your strategy is taking one or two elements of your strategy as a starting point and from there on innovate the rest of your strategy. This 'routed innovation' approach is particularly useful in three situations:

A If you have no idea where to start once you have mapped out your strategy using the Strategy Sketch. Choosing one clear starting point makes sure you don't get lost in all the possibilities of strategic innovation.

B If you have a clear idea what you want to keep or find important as part of your new strategy. In that case you can take that element as a starting point for innovation.

C If you want to deliberately work from different perspectives when innovating your strategy. This would imply you start at one point and switch to another and in the end combine the insights gained as such.

There are six basic routes that you can follow or combine for this approach to strategic innovation.

### 1 Market-driven strategy

The first and most well-known starting point is to start with an analysis of the market to find out the needs of (potential) customers, and to assess the extent and nature of the competition. This approach is also known as the 'outside-in approach' to strategy. Using the Strategy Sketch, it starts with mapping your customers and needs and competitors. From thereon, the rest of the strategy can be sketched by asking questions such as: "What kind of new or additional products, services, or features would customers value?" "How can we differentiate ourselves better from competitors?" and "What kind of resources or competences do we need in order to do that?"

### 2 Means-driven strategy

A second route is to start on the other side of the Strategy Sketch, with the organization's resources and competences and partners. This 'means-driven strategy' is also known as the 'inside-out approach' to strategy. Means-driven strategy starts with inventorying the current strengths and weaknesses of the organization: What means (money, materials, machines, people, knowledge, etc.) does the organization have and does it have access to through its partners. Subsequent questions are "How unique and valuable are these means compared to competitors?" "What kind of products or services can we develop based on these means?" or "How can we use the available means better?"

### 3 Identity-driven strategy

You can also start innovating your strategy based on the organization's identity; what it stands for and what it aims to achieve. This route starts with making the mission and vision of the organization clear and expressing what goals and values are important. This route is closely linked to the people that work for the organization and the culture that binds them together. In the Strategy Sketch this relates to the elements of values and goals and organizational climate. Typical follow-up questions are "What kind of customers do we find important to serve?" "What kind of business do we want to be?" and "What kind of competences do we need in order to achieve our goals?"

4 **Revenue-driven strategy**
A fourth innovation route is to focus on maximizing revenue and minimizing costs and risks. This 'revenue-driven' strategy aims at maximizing the financial returns of a business – making a profit. This route takes the revenue model and risks and costs elements as starting points. From thereon, questions that can be asked are: "What kind of market would enable us to maximize our returns?" "How can we minimize the risks of our business?" or "What portfolio of products and services would we need to obtain a balance between risks and returns?"

5 **Context-driven strategy**
The fifth route is more responsive and opportunistic. It takes the trends and uncertainties that arise in the organization's environment as the main starting point. Organizations following this approach try to make the best of the situation they are in by exploiting trends or avoiding and dealing with the uncertainties they face. Relevant questions for this approach include: "How can we make best use of the situation we are in now?" "How should we respond to important trends in society?" and "What kind of products or services could we come up with to make use of these trends?"

"There are three factors that make one route more logical than another."

6 **Value proposition-driven strategy**
A final route for innovating your strategy is to start directly with your value proposition rather than taking any of the other elements as a starting point. With this route you try to come up with improvements to your value proposition or with a completely new value proposition. This is the core of Blue ocean strategy which I already referred to in the 'Useful models' section for the value proposition in Chapter 4 (page 81). When you follow this innovation route you take your own value proposition, or the average value proposition as it is offered in the industry as a starting point. You then look at which features can be created, raised, reduced, or eliminated.

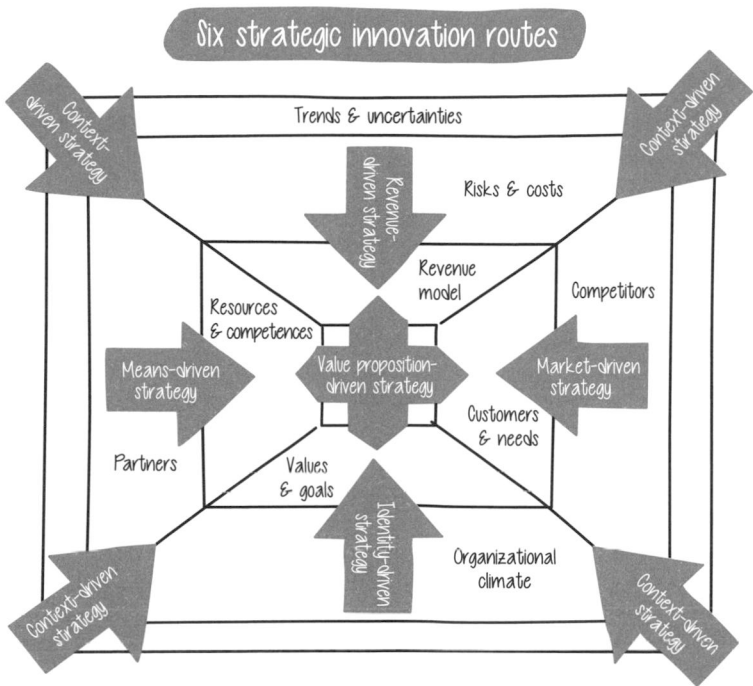

Six strategic innovation routes

Trends & uncertainties

Context-driven strategy

Context-driven strategy

Revenue-driven strategy

Risks & costs

Revenue model

Competitors

Resources & competences

Means-driven strategy

Value proposition-driven strategy

Market-driven strategy

Customers & needs

Partners

Values & goals

Identity-driven strategy

Organizational climate

Context-driven strategy

Context-driven strategy

## Which innovation route to choose?

I can imagine that you are wondering which of these six innovation routes you should choose. The short and not so helpful answer to this question is: Whichever you want. There is some truth in this answer though, as there is no best starting point and in the end it is up to you where you choose to start. Also, you can always start in different places and see what works best for you. You might even want to combine a few or even all of them throughout the strategy generation process.

However, there are at least three factors that make one route more logical than another. Therefore, in choosing between routes you might want to take the following three factors into account:

① The outcomes of the previous step – the *assessment* of your strategy. If, for example, the assessment shows inefficiencies in the way you use your resources and competences, it would be quite logical to start with a means-driven innovation route here. Or, if your organizational climate or revenue model are

151

not flexible or robust you might want to follow, respectively, the identity-driven or the revenue-driven route.

2. The *uncertainty* of the market or industry you are in. If you are in a very uncertain environment – such as a new or dynamic industry or a complex market – relying on customer needs or on trends can be a bit tricky. If things are so uncertain, you simply cannot know whether the needs and trends that you identify will be true or relevant. The only thing you can rely on in these situations is who you are and what you have. Therefore, in these situations the means-driven and identity-driven routes are more suitable than a market-driven or context-driven route.

3. The strength of your *values and goals*. If you have a clear idea of what you find important and where you want to go with the organization, the obvious innovation route is the identify-driven route. In this case you may want to start by formulating a clear and compelling vision and mission from which you then derive the other elements of your strategy.

# Innovation approach 4: Projective innovation

All three previous approaches aim at improving and innovating your *current* strategy. This means that, in one way or the other, they all take your existing strategy as a starting point. Projective innovation, on the other hand, starts with projecting one or more possible futures and from thereon deriving what strategy would be suitable for dealing with these futures. This approach can help you look at your strategy in a new way and come up with more radically new and future-proof strategies.

A useful tool for this innovation approach is the PESTLE analysis, which I mentioned in the 'Useful models' section for the trends and uncertainties element in Chapter 4 (page 99). You can use that tool as a checklist for sensing trends and uncertainties that have an immediate or short-term effect on your strategy. That was the kind of application I had in mind there. However, you can also use a PESTLE analysis to project what the world or your industry could look like in the long term – in let's say five, ten, or twenty years. And this is what I have in mind here. Projective innovation requires the following three steps:

1 **Identify megatrends**
Start by identifying the important political, economic, social, technological, legal, and environmental trends that are happening. You should focus on what are called 'structural developments' or 'megatrends' – those trends that are relatively certain and that will probably go on for quite a while. Think of, for example, important demographic or technological changes that are happening. When you identify these trends, you shouldn't let yourself be too restricted by the PESTLE categories. Use them as a checklist, but don't necessarily stick to them. Also, you can use the websites of the World Future Society (www.wfs.org), the Copenhagen Institute for Future Studies (www.cifs.dk), the World Futures Studies Federation (www.wfsf.org), or other websites like this for insights into the future.

2 **Sketch one or more possible futures**
Once you have a good sense of these megatrends use them to sketch what your relevant world would look like in five, ten, or twenty years. So, try to picture, for instance, what your industry will look like or in what kind of world your future customer will be living ten years from now. For this it can be quite useful to make an Empathy map (which was introduced in the Beyond-the-obvious exercise for customers and needs in Chapter 4 on page 72). Generating this picture (or pictures if you want) should give you a lot of inspiration as to what your future strategy could look like.

3 **Derive implications for your strategy**
The final step is to identify what the picture you developed means for your strategy. This means you should try to come up with a strategy that would be suitable for the future you have projected. For this you can again use the Strategy Sketch and its ten elements. Thus, you identify what kind of resources and competences you would need, what kind of partners, who your competitors could be, and so on.

With just three steps, this is a simple way to use the projective innovation approach. If you want, you can go much deeper and make your innovation process much more comprehensive. If you choose to do so, I recommend you read more on topics such as futures studies, forecasting, and scenario planning (see page 100 for a brief summary of the latter).

# Step 4

## Innovation approach 5: Freestyle innovation

Do you want to go even wilder and come up with some crazy ideas for your strategy? In that case freestyle strategic innovation is a suitable approach. Whereas the other four approaches assume some boundaries to your innovation freedom, you drop these with freestyle innovation. This fifth type of strategic innovation is especially useful in the following cases:

- **(A)** If you want to come up with a strategy that is really new and could lead to a whole new market. Through freestyle innovation you might get ideas that you otherwise would not have had.
- **(B)** If you want to depart from your current strategy and do something very different than you currently do. The other approaches might make it too tempting to stay within your comfort zone.
- **(C)** If you want to stimulate creativity within a phase of the strategy generation process. You don't want to actually do something radically new, but some of the crazy ideas might be useful when toned down.

> "This approach can help you look at your strategy in a new way and come up with more radically new and future-proof strategies."

The basic idea of freestyle strategic innovation is that you challenge yourself to take your strategy to extreme situations. This is done by a variety of 'What if...' scenarios. The goal is not necessarily to develop complete strategies, but to come up with new ideas.

### Thirty 'What if...' scenarios

Below you will find thirty very short scenarios that can help you think about your strategy in an unconventional manner. The idea is that you pick one scenario at a time and imagine what your strategy might look like in that scenario. As with other brainstorming techniques it is important that everything is possible and that no objections are allowed throughout the idea generation process. You can repeat this process multiple times with different scenarios. So, here are the scenarios: What would your strategy look like if...

1. ...you started completely from scratch without any limitations or constrains *(Greenfield scenario).*
2. ...you cut out anything you don't like or which is hindering you in realizing your ambitions *(Weeds scenario).*
3. ...there were a fire and you could only save your single most precious resource *(Fire scenario).*
4. ...you had to double your revenue without hiring anyone or buying anything for two years *(Multiply scenario).*
5. ...you had to cut your expenses and staff by half without reducing your revenue *(Diet scenario).*
6. ...you had to do everything online - or offline if you're a web-based organization *(Online / offline scenario).*
7. ...you had to run the organization from a bus or camper traveling across the globe *(Mobile scenario).*
8. ...you had to outsource virtually everything that is done by the organization *(Outsourcing scenario).*
9. ...you were required to achieve at least 80% of the current results with no more than 20% of the current effort *(80/20 scenario).*
10. ...your customers had just one tenth to spend of what they normally have *(Poor man's scenario).*
11. ...you had to sell your products or services for a price ten times higher than normal *(Rich man's scenario).*
12. ...you had to make sure customers queued overnight to buy your product or service *(Wow scenario).*
13. ...customers asked for something entirely different every year *(Changing tastes scenario).*
14. ...you switched from products to services as your primary focus or the other way around *(Product/service scenario).*
15. ...you were to win the Nobel Peace Prize, solve world poverty, or stop climate change *(World peace scenario).*
16. ...you moved to the most exotic, dangerous, or unique country you know *(Adventurer's scenario).*
17. ...money didn't exist and you exclusively relied on barter and in-kind payments (payment by goods or services) *(Barter scenario).*
18. ...your organization were ten or even a hundred times larger *(Explosion scenario).*
19. ...you copied the best ideas from the best organizations you know *(Aping scenario).*
20. ...there suddenly appeared an exact copy of your organization *(Copycat scenario).*

(21) ...employees made the decisions instead of managers or directors *(Employee scenario)*.

(22) ...your grandma, grandson, or uncle was running the organization *(Family scenario)*.

(23) ...your accountant, lawyer, supplier, customer, consultant took over *(Partner scenario)*.

(24) ...Richard Branson, Michael O'Leary, Steve Jobs, Walt Disney, Henry Ford, Warren Buffett, or Bill Gates took over *(Star entrepreneur scenario)*.

(25) ...Jesus, Mother Theresa, Martin Luther King, the Dalai Lama, Mohamed, or Buddha was running the organization *(Compassion scenario)*.

(26) ...you merged with the most unlikely organization you can imagine *(Unlikely marriage scenario)*.

(27) ...you were alive 10, 100, or 1000 years from now or 10, 100, or 1000 years ago *(Time traveller scenario)*.

(28) ...the market grew each year by at least 20% *(Optimist scenario)*.

(29) ...the market decreased each year by at least 20% *(Pessimist scenario)*.

(30) ...you just followed your intuitions or instincts even though you cannot justify them *(Guts scenario)*.

Of course you don't need to restrict yourself to these scenarios. Any other scenario that takes you out of the normal is also appropriate.

# Generating and selecting strategic options

All these five innovation approaches aim at finding and developing new ideas for your strategy. New ideas, though, are not complete strategies yet. And you might even have plenty of ideas between which you need to make a choice. This means that some additional work may be needed before you can move on to the last step – Formulating strategy. Two follow-up steps are usually required: Turning the idea into a complete strategy, and choosing between various options.

1 **Turning an idea into a complete strategy**
As argued in Chapter 2, the Strategy Sketch contains all the important elements of a strategy. Therefore, I don't think you will

be surprised if I recommend you use the Strategy Sketch to turn your ideas into complete strategies. So what you do is the following: For the idea that you have come up with, map out all the necessary elements. In other words, go back to the mapping step and map out an entire strategy around the idea. Suppose, for example, you have come up with an idea for a new value proposition. You then map out what customers and needs it would serve, who your competitors are, what resources and competences and partners you would need, and so on.

"As a rule of thumb, if you have more than three ideas, it is useful to first make a quick assessment aimed at filtering out the best three."

2 **Choosing between optional strategies**

There is a big chance that you have come up with multiple ideas for a new strategy. Since you can't execute all of them, you must somehow choose between them. What you need for this is a way of comparing and assessing the various ideas that you have generated. To do this, you go back to the previous step of the strategy generation process – assessing strategy. Instead of assessing a single strategy, you assess the various options that you have generated and compare them.

There is no strict order for these two follow-up steps. Sometimes you could immediately assess your ideas before turning them into complete strategies, and sometimes you first want to develop them further before you go to assess them. As a rule of thumb, if you have more than three ideas, it is useful to first make a quick assessment aimed at filtering out the best three. Next, turn these ideas into complete strategies and assess them more systematically.

# The**four**examples

**Note**: *these two pages describe the strategic innovation approach of the four examples. See the next chapter for the outcomes.*

## Strategic innovation at Macman

As the assessment shows, Macman's main strategic issues are insufficient flexibility and efficiency. Furthermore, its leadership has a hard time imagining feasible alternatives. This makes freestyle innovation suitable, as it encourages generating unconventional ideas. The following two scenarios are particularly appropriate:

- **Outsourcing scenario** ("what if you had to outsource virtually everything that is done by the organization?"). This scenario helps them think about a more flexible strategy based on collaboration rather than on doing everything in-house.
- **Wow scenario** ("what if you had to make sure customers queued overnight to buy your product or service?"). This scenario helps them put themselves in their customers' shoes and realize what additional needs they could fulfill.

## Strategic innovation at Hospicare

Hospicare's main strategy issues were a lack of effectiveness and coherence. Furthermore, the board needed to be convinced that new strategy was unavoidable and advantageous. In this case a combination of routed and freestyle innovation works well:

- **Routed innovation.** Hospicare has a strong and distinctive climate and competence: They are very businesslike and focused on successful operations. They can use this as a starting point for means-driven and identity-driven innovation. The question here is how these features of Hospicare can be used better.
- **Freestyle innovation,** using the Wow scenario (see Macman) or the Employee scenario ("what if employees made the decisions instead of managers or directors?"). These scenarios force Hospicare to think about effectiveness from the view of their customers and employees.

## Strategic innovation at GoforIT

The assessment of GoforIT's strategy showed that they have no unique resources that hinder competitors from copying them, and that they could do more in terms of responsibility.

For the first issue, elementary innovation is suitable. Zooming in on the resources and competence element, the key point is what GoforIT can do to avoid imitation. The questions from the uniqueness check are helpful for this. The copycat scenario ("what if there suddenly appeared an exact copy of your organization?") is also suitable.

With respect to responsibility, GoforIT's founders need to be made aware of the possibility and appropriateness of letting others than themselves benefit from the company's success. The following freestyle innovation scenarios are helpful in achieving this:

- **World peace scenario** ("what if you were to win the Nobel Peace Prize, solve world poverty, or stop climate change?").
- **Compassion scenario** ("what if Jesus, Mother Theresa, Martin Luther King, etc. were running the organization?").

## Strategic innovation at Comcom

Anisha's problem is that Comcom's strategy is not unique and scalable and that she doesn't see the ways to make it so. At the same time she has a dream of having a famous food blog for which it is unclear whether and when it could generate income.

With respect to the scalability of her current business, amplifying innovation is the obvious choice. In order to make her strategy more scalable she is recommended to apply all the scalability tactics to her company and see which ones she can use.

Once that succeeds she will be able to spend more time on her dream (a famous food blog) in parallel. If the blog attracts a lot of readers, that will be the time to think about how to generate revenue.

# 7 Formulating strategy

This chapter explains the last step of the strategy generation process: Formulating strategy. In this fifth step you turn your newly developed strategy into a form that can be communicated to others. As such, this step closes the strategy generation process so that you can turn to strategy execution again. This chapter starts with an explanation of what strategy formulation entails. It then presents various forms in which you could formulate your strategy using words and pictures.

> Formulating Strategy:
> **Capturing the organization's strategy in words and pictures that can be understood by the target audience.**

## The strategy formulation challenge

If you were successful in the previous steps, you now have one or more new strategic ideas that you have turned into more or less complete Strategy Sketches. This means you have gathered and produced all the important ingredients of your new strategy. However, it would be a stretch to already call this your strategy. You have a *sketch* of your strategy and its key elements, but this still needs to be turned into something concise that can be communicated to others. Only then can you actually tell people what your strategy is – what your unique way of sustainable value creation is. Thus, the key challenge of strategy formulation is generating an answer to the question of what your strategy is.

If you look it up in the strategy literature, you'll find that the expression strategy formulation is oftentimes used to capture the entire strategy generation process. This suggests that generating new strategy is merely a matter of formulating it. As you know by now, however, strategy generation involves much more than that, and actually formulating the strategy is 'only' the last step.

In the first section of Chapter 3, 'The activation challenge', we saw that the purpose of the activation step is getting the organization from a strategy execution mode into a strategy generation mode. The purpose of strategy formulation is exactly the opposite: Getting the organization back into execution mode. By formulating the strategy, you close the strategy generation process – at least for a while – so that the organization can focus on its execution.

## "The purpose of strategy formulation is getting the organization back into execution mode."

### Roles of strategy formulation

In line with this overall purpose, strategy formulation plays several specific roles in the strategy generation process – I found at least six of them. Since these roles affect how you should precisely formulate your strategy, it is useful to keep in mind which of them you are focusing on. The roles are:

- **Refining:** In order to formulate your strategy you need to make it concrete. And as soon as you make it concrete you will also see whether your strategy is as crisp and good as you thought, or whether it still requires refinement. Thus, a first role of strategy formulation is that it helps refine your strategy.

- **Fixating:** Centered on the idea of the Strategy Sketch, the previous steps reflect a creative and dynamic process that facilitates idea generation and frequent adjustments to your strategy. This is good for strategy generation, but at some point you will want to fixate your strategy as well. Strategy formulation serves this role.

- **Convincing:** To get the strategy going, you need to get people involved and committed. This means you may need to convince quite a few people of the strengths and importance of your strategy – such as employees, investors, or the board of directors. Quite obviously, strategy formulation plays a crucial role in this.

- **Driving:** As research in cognitive psychology shows, the simple act of making something concrete forms an enormous stimulus to actually doing it – seeing is believing. This applies to strategy as well: Formulating it in a concrete manner makes people believe in the feasibility of a strategy. As such, strategy formulation drives the execution of a strategy.

- **Acting:** Formulating strategy also helps turn the strategy into concrete actions and plans. A well-formulated strategy expresses not only what the strategy is, but also why it works and what it takes. As such, it gives a clear idea of the required actions for the organization.

- **Signaling:** Strategy formulation can also serve as a subtle (or less subtle) means of communicating to others, such as competitors. It can serve as a warning or an announcement to show them what your plans are or that you are serious. Some bluffing and misleading may be part of this.

## Your target audience

When we look at these six roles, we can immediately see that it also matters for strategy formulation who your target audience is. If you formulate your strategy, for example, to convince investors, you will probably want to emphasize different things than when you formulate it for refining it with the management team, or for driving your employees towards strategy execution. This means that, when formulating your strategy, you should also take into account who you are formulating it for. You should think of at least the following target audiences:

- The management team, strategy officers, business developers, or others involved in strategy generation.
- Employees, middle managers, or others that are involved in the execution of the strategy.
- The board of directors, the CEO, shareholders, or others that have to formally approve the strategy.
- Investors, banks, or others from which you need investments or guarantees.

- Customers, suppliers, partners, or other external parties that are needed for a strategy to become successful.
- Competitors, media, or other external parties that you want to make your strategy known to.

To sum up, the challenge of strategy formulation is to express your strategy in such a way that it fulfills the particular role that you want to a particular target audience.

# The core and structure of your strategy

When I ask people to tell me the strategy of their organization I get surprisingly different and unsatisfying answers. Some argue it is 'operational excellence' or 'customer intimacy' or they provide a description of their core products or of their unique competences. Others give a rather abstract mission or vision statement, or an objective such as growth or consolidation. Still others refer to their strategic plan or they are unable to provide an answer at all.

This variety of answers shows two things: First, that there is no single right aspect to focus on when formulating strategy, and second that there is a lot of room for improvement as to how strategy is formulated. These two refer, respectively, to the core of the formulated strategy (what the key point you are trying to make is) and its structure (how you tell it in a clear and convincing manner).

## The core of the formulated strategy

The variety of answers described above indicates that people choose to focus on very different aspects of strategy when they formulate it. We could try to harmonize this and suggest a one-size-fits all recipe for how to correctly formulate a strategy. I don't think that is a very fruitful path though, as it limits your ability to express a unique strategy. And why would it be wrong if you focus on your competences, while others focus on their value proposition, goals, or anything else?

# "When formulating strategy you need to make a choice as to what will be the core of your message."

Throughout the previous steps we have worked with the ten key elements of strategy. So far, we have treated these ten elements as more or less equal. Whether it is in the mapping, assessing, or innovating step, there was no hierarchy among these elements. Of course, I showed you my preferred order of mapping the elements. But that is just my preference, not a law. And it doesn't mean at all that one element should be emphasized more in your strategy than any other. For these three steps it works very well not to prioritize one element over the other. You need to think about all of them, and putting one above the others during that stage can already seriously restrict the creativity and openness that you need during strategy generation.

However, when formulating strategy you need to decide what will be the core of your message. Your strategy won't be very appealing if you just list the ten elements without any particular emphasis on any of them. Therefore, you want to pick one as your core and use the rest to support it.

Maybe not all the elements are equally well suited to forming the core of your strategy formulation. The trends and uncertainties, for example, seem less suitable than your value proposition or values and goals because they refer more to the environment you're in than your actual strategy. However, as we will see further on in this chapter, each of them can be used as a core.

## The structure of the formulated strategy

Once you have picked your core element the next step is to build a clear and convincing reasoning that explains why and how your strategy is a good one. Just stating, for example, your value proposition or your values and goals is nice, but it is not sufficient to fulfill any of the six roles identified above. Whether you want to refine or fixate your strategy, convince or drive people, make them act, or signal something, you need to say more than that.

# "A well-formulated strategy covers all ten elements of the Strategy Sketch."

A well-formulated strategy covers all ten elements of the Strategy Sketch. After all, they are the ten key elements, and if you could do without them in your strategy formulation, they wouldn't be very key, would they? This means that you should use the other nine elements to support the core of your strategy. Thus, if your core is your value proposition, use your customers and needs to explain that there is a market for your value proposition, your competitors for explaining how it is different from what they are doing, your resources and competences for explaining what makes you able to realize it, and so on. The remainder of this chapter shows you how to do this.

## Formulating strategy in words

The most obvious way of formulating your strategy is to turn it into words, usually in the form of some written document. The challenge is to find a way of formulating that has the right length, structure, and level of detail. On the one hand a strategy text should be clear and precise enough to express the strategy in sufficient detail to understand it. On the other hand you also want it to be as concise as possible. The next few pages present three steps for doing this.

## 1 Capture the core

The first thing you want to do is to pick the core element of your strategy. This can be any of the ten elements; there are no clear rules for making this choice. You might have a personal preference, or the organization might have chosen a particular focus already in formulating the current strategy. Or maybe, during the previous steps, you found that one particular element clearly stood out in terms of importance. In all these cases it might be fairly straightforward as to what the core of your strategy should be. In other cases, though, you might do the following exercise to pick the core of your strategy:

1 Let everyone involved in the strategy generation process (or a selection of them) summarize the strategy in one simple sentence. You can let them write this freely, but you could also force them to start the sentence with "Our strategy is ..."

2 Share the sentences with everyone, vote and pick the best. You probably don't want to just use a majority vote, but also discuss the different formulations and come to an agreement.

3 Look at which of the ten elements is best captured in the sentence that was chosen. You now have your core.

## "Try to capture the core element of your strategy in a single sentence."

Instead of starting with a variety of sentences at the first step, you could also start with one and then iterate. This means that you or someone else writes a first version of the sentence, and others modify it as they like. The risk with this approach though, is that this leads to endless changes and a not-so-inspiring process. Therefore, I personally prefer the above exercise.

To support this exercise you can also give examples of how the core of the strategy can be captured in a single sentence. Maybe you know a good example of another organization, but you can also use the following list of ten generic examples, starting with...

1 **Resources & competences.** You present your unique strengths that differentiate you from your competitors.
*Example format:* Our strategy is to build on and further develop these, as well as these means and our ability to do such and such.

2 **Partners.** You present who you work with and the collaborations that give you a unique position.
*Example format:* Our strategy is to work with these as well as these partners and to use our unique network in such and such way.

3 **Customers & needs.** You define your main customers and thus for whom the organization does what it does.

*Example format:* Our strategy is to be the preferred supplier of choice for this and this group of customers.

4 **Competitors.** You define who your main competitors are and what you aim to achieve with respect to them.
*Example format:* Our strategy is to be the best such and such in this as well as this industry or region.

5 **Value proposition.** You point out what you offer in terms of products, services, and their added value.
*Example format:* Our strategy is to offer such and such products or services that stand out in terms of these and these features.

6 **Revenue model.** You explain what your most important sources of revenue are and where they come from.
*Example format:* Our strategy is to earn our money in such and such way or to offer our products/services in return for such and such a fee.

7 **Risks & costs.** You explain how you deal with risks and costs and how that makes you stand out compared to others.
*Example format:* Our strategy is to minimize these risks and costs by dealing with them in such and such ways.

8 **Values & goals.** You state what you want to achieve and/or what is of key importance for the organization.
*Example format:* Our strategy is to achieve this and this by that and that time, or to serve this and this purpose.

9 **Organizational climate.** You point out what kind of organization you are and what is unique about it.
*Example format:* Our strategy is to be such and such an organization or an organization characterized by such and such a structure or culture.

10 **Trends & uncertainties.** Your present some key trends or uncertainties in your environment and how you deal with them.
*Example format:* Our strategy is to jump on these and these trends or to deal with these and these uncertainties in this and this way.

> **Note:** *It is not always strictly necessary to pick just one of the ten elements as your core. Maybe you have two that you want to combine. However, I would recommend you to stick to one or two because otherwise it is not really a core anymore and your formulation might become diffuse.*

## 2 Build up the reasoning

After the first step you have captured the essence of your strategy. This is important and it might already give a lot of clarity as to what your strategy is. Next, in order to make it convincing, you also want to explain in more detail why it is a good strategy and what it is based on. For this you want to build up a reasoning that includes the other elements of your strategy.

So, what you need to do is to build up a logical chain of reasoning whereby you connect the other nine elements to the core of your strategy. There is no single best order for doing that. On the other hand, with ten elements and ten different starting points there are over three million possible orders (3,628,800 to be precise), which are not equally suitable. Therefore, I will just share with you three templates that have different but equally convincing logics for formulating your strategy.

"Build up a logical chain of reasoning whereby you connect the other nine elements to the core of your strategy."

## Example template 1: Means-based template

### Our strategy is to...
Build on and further develop these and these means and our ability to do such and such *{Resources & competences}* ...

We do this with these and these *{Partners}* ...
And an organization that is characterized by *{Organizational climate}* ...

These starting points give us an advantage compared to *{Competitors}* ...
In an environment which is characterized by *{Trends & uncertainties}* ...

Based on this we offer *{Value proposition}* ...
To address these and these *{Customers & needs}* ...

We make this viable by this and this *{Revenue model}* ...
And by dealing in this and this way with our *{Risk & costs}* ...

By doing so we reach *{Values & goals}* ...

## Example template 2: Identity-based template

### Our strategy is to...
Achieve this and this by that and that time or to serve this and this purpose {Values & goals} ...
With an organization that is characterized by *{Organizational climate}* ...

We do this by offering *{Value proposition}* ...
To address these and these *{Customers & needs}* ...

In an environment which is characterized by *{Trends & uncertainties}* ...
We can do this better than *{Competitors}* ...

Because we have *{Resources & competences}* ...
And because we work with *{Partners}* ...

This is viable through this and this *{Revenue model}* ...
And through this and this way of dealing with *{Risk & costs}* ...

## Example template 3: Market-based template

### Our strategy is to...

Be the preferred supplier of choice for this and this group of customers *{Customers & needs}* ...

In an environment that is characterized by these *{Trends & uncertainties}* ...
We achieve this by offering this and this *{Value proposition}* ...
By which we distinguish ourselves from *{Competitors}* ...

By doing so we reach *{Values & goals}* ...

This is viable through *{Revenue model}* ...
And through dealing in such and such a way with *{Risk & costs}* ...

We can do this because we have *{Resources & competences}* ...
Because we have *{Organizational climate}* ...
And because we work with *{Partners}* ...

If you feel too restricted by these templates, you should definitely take the opportunity to adjust them and depart from the wording that is suggested. These three templates just serve as examples to get you started. As long as you make sure that you cover the ten elements in your reasoning, you should choose whatever structure and way of formulating works best for you. Furthermore, as suggested at the beginning of this chapter, you should also keep in mind who you are addressing (your target audience) and what you are trying to achieve (the roles of strategy formulation).

## 3 Choose a format and length

After that you have captured the core of your strategy and built up a convincing reasoning to support it, the last step is to choose an appropriate format and length that serves your purpose. You might want to consider one or more of the following formats:

1 **A one-pager.** A brief summary of your strategy on one side of a single sheet of paper. In this format you use a couple of sentences to capture each element of your strategy along the lines of the

templates above. You should try to write densely and thus limit the number of unnecessary and connecting phrases.

2   **A five to ten page report.** This should contain the same message and structure as the one-pager, but amended with proof. While the one-pager provides the logic and reasoning for your strategy, this reports adds evidence and further explanations that might be needed to convince people of your strategy.

3   **A single slide.** When you need to pitch your strategy in a couple of minutes, you don't want full sentences and even a one-pager is too long. In that case you might want to prepare a single slide that covers your strategy in 5-7 bullet points.

4   **A short slide deck.** If you have time for a longer presentation, you could prepare a slide deck of about ten slides explaining your strategy. Like in the report above, you also have some room to include evidence to convince your audience.

# The**four**examples

Based on our four examples, you find four ways of formulating strategy below. You should keep in mind that they are not necessarily good strategies or the best way of formulating them. However, these examples are meant to show you the various ways in which you could formulate your strategy by covering the elements of the Strategy Sketch, without ending up with some mechanical list of those elements.

## Macman's strategy

**Note:** *Macman had issues with the flexibility and efficiency of their strategy and were looking for the next big idea. To solve most of these issues, they decided to offer complementary machines and services to the customers of their existing products. They aimed at formulating a brief summary of their strategy that can be shared with all employees so that everybody in the organization understands and knows it. This is their attempt (of course without the elements in brackets:*

In a globalizing market in which the number and sophistication of competitors grows and competition is increasingly price-based *{trends & uncertainties}*, our strategy is to distinguish ourselves from other steel cutting and bending manufacturers and particularly from companies X, Y, and Z *{competitors}*, by offering not only steel cutting and bending machines, but also complementary machines and personalized services *{value proposition}* so that our customers – high-precision machine manufacturers in Europe – are relieved of all concerns regarding their machine park *{customers & needs}*.

By doing so we are able to maintain our current size and market share, while increasing our profitability and offering our employees a challenging and comfortable working environment *{values & goals}*. This is viable because our service level and complementary products allow us to charge a premium price above the market average *{revenue model}* and because we have a zero waste policy and outsource the production of complementary products *{risks & costs}*.

173

We are able to do this primarily because we excel at translating customer needs into machine specifications *{resources & competences}*, because we are the industry's best employer for the past 3 years and are able to attract the most skilled engineers in the world *{organizational climate}*, and because we closely collaborate with companies A, B, and C, which produce all complementary products and with our steel suppliers *{partners}*.

## Hospicare's strategy

*Note: Hospicare decided to start with a small pilot to commercialize their knowledge of psychiatric problems and their treatment. For this they aim at setting up a new company outside the hospital. They formulate their strategy as follows:*

### Our vision

Ten years from now our hospital will have a hub-and-spoke model with a hospital at the core, surrounded by at least ten private, specialized health centers *{values & goals}*.

### Our mission

We offer affordable, reliable, and no-nonsense treatments for people with psychiatric and orthopedic problems and diseases *{values & goals}*.

### Our strategy

Our market is changing. Increasing regulations and decreasing health insurance coverage mean that more and more people need to pay personally for parts of their health care *{trends & uncertainties}*. We respond to this trend by gradually moving away from insurance-based health care to offering low-cost, standardized commercial health-care services for patients with psychiatric or orthopedic problems *{revenue model, value proposition, and customers & needs}*.

We aim to do this in the form of a hub-and-spokes model with our current hospital at the core, and small, private health centers as satellites around it. This model provides us with an excellent network of specialized partners that helps us brand our services, share capacity, and mutual learning *{partners}*.

We are able to deliver high quality at low prices because of a) our excellent knowledge of psychiatric and orthopedic problems and disorders *{resources & competences}*; b) our cost-efficient standardized, and lean processes *{resources & competences, risks & costs}*; and c) our professional, business-like and no-nonsense culture and way of working *{organizational climate}*.

No other hospital in our region will be able to mimic our approach in the short or medium-term because none of them has a similar business-like way of working *{competitors}*.

## GoforIT's strategy

*Note: The assessment of GoforIT's strategy showed some issues with the uniqueness of their competences and regarding the sharing of their wealth with employees. However, the founders decided they first need to grow further before addressing those issues. To do so, they want a financial injection from a venture capitalist. As a starting point for a presentation, they prepared a single slide. In just five bullet points they cover the essence of their strategy, thereby paying attention to almost all the elements.*

### GoforIT's strategy for the next two years

- **Our unique product:** Financial software and apps that are intuitive for financial people, IT-ers, and managers
- **Who the competition is:** Companies R, T, and Z + other companies offering free or paid financial software
- **Why we're better than others:** We have employees with these three types of backgrounds (one-third each) + a process in which they work effectively together + our brand.
- **Where the market is going:** A growing number of small businesses, combined with a decreasing willingness to pay → we need to scale up!
- **How we can still make money:** If sales numbers triple, costs increase marginally. Price of products can drop by 50%

**Conclusion: if we can triple our sales in the next two years, we can maintain our position and remain very profitable**

## Comcom's strategy

*Note: Since Anisha is on her own and doesn't need any money from a bank or any other source, she only needs to formulate the strategy for herself, so that it is clear for her what her strategy is. She wanted to make her strategy more scalable so that she had to spend less time on her current business while earning the same amount of money.*

➔ My dream: To write a food blog that is read by thousands of people.

➔ The 'organization' that I need to realize this dream: Just me, having fun while working and with a good work-life balance/mix.

➔ My concrete offer that helps me realize the dream:
  1. Standardized communication services based on predefined templates. Affordable for the client + easy and low-cost for me.
  2. Food blog with interesting news and information about food. First to gain traffic, later on to earn a living.

➔ The clients that will buy and use what I offer:
  1. Accountancy firms (still the largest group, and I need an income, but I won't make any additional acquisition efforts).
  2. Amateur and lower-level professional cooks (target group) + people interested in food (also nice, but a bit broad).

➔ Who are my most important competitors:
  1. The many other communication services and advisors.
  2. Other food blogs and websites, both national and international.

➔ Why and with whom I will beat them:
  1. Communication services: I will beat them by price through my smart standardizes templates!
  2. Food blog: Not sure whether I can 'beat' the others, but I do have a fun and entertaining way of writing that I know others like. Also, I have quite a good network with chefs of excellent restaurants that are willing to help.

➤ How I make my money:
  1 Fixed price per service; can be low-priced and still profitable because of the templates I use. Also, it leaves me time to start the food blog.
  2 At the start not yet; once I have traffic I will use advertising. I could also sell related products such as recipe books, tools and so on, but we'll see whether that is going to happen (maybe even a book based on the blogs?). Costs are low (free Wordpress site, cheap hosting + my time).

➤ What could happen? I have no idea, and to be honest I don't really care too much. Currently people seem to be interested in food, especially healthy food, but I don't know whether this will stay that way. I am just going to make this work and will jump at new opportunities when they arise.

# Formulating strategy in pictures

Next to formulating your strategy in words, you can also formulate it visually, through images, figures, movies, and the like. Along with the saying that a picture is worth a thousand words, it sometimes may be more effective to formulate strategy in this way than with words. I don't think this can really replace formulating your strategy in words – you'll mostly need to do that anyway – but as a complementary way of formulating it, it can certainly be very valuable.

## It is about the message, not about the looks

It is great if you have the skills to visualize your strategy into an advanced, stylish, or cool image, or if you can hire people who can do this. However, that is not the real point here. Form matters, of course. However, it is far more important *what* you formulate and that people get it, than whether it looks great or not. Therefore, don't let a supposed lack of graphical skills be a barrier against visualizing your strategy.

There are unlimited ways in which you can make your strategy visual, and any way is suitable as long as it expresses the strategy in a way that is understood by your target audience. If you already have a form in mind; great, than don't let the following few pages restrict your creativity. Skip them and move on. If you need some suggestions, though, you might think of the following four options.

| Type of visualization | Great for |
| --- | --- |
| Storyboard or whiteboard animation | Expressing the *core* of your strategy |
| Visual strategy sketch | Expressing the *structure* of your strategy |
| Causal map | Expressing the *causal logic* of your strategy |
| Strategy roadmap | Expressing how strategy unfolds over *time* |

## Storyboard or whiteboard animation

When making a storyboard of your strategy you turn it into a visual, cartoon-like story, which shows the core of your strategy. A whiteboard animation does the same, but it is a recording of the drawing process supported by a voice-over and optional sound effects that tell the story. This visualization is great for sharing the essence of your strategy in a simple and energizing way. It helps make your strategy concrete so that you can identify possible problems before actually executing it. There are two basic forms:

**Freeform:** Just start on a plain whiteboard and build up a picture that tells the story of your strategy. There is also software available for this – just search for 'whiteboard animation software.'

**Storyboard:** Divide your whiteboard into four to six boxes and tell a cartoon-like story in simple pictures. Two ways to divide your story between the boxes include, but are certainly not limited to:
- What you offer (value proposition), to whom (customer and needs), what you get in return (revenue model), and who your unhappy competitors are (competitors).
- What you want to achieve (values and goals), what you need for that (resources and competences), with what kind of organization (organizational climate), and what kind of partners (partners).

Hospicare's strategy

# Step 5

## Visual strategy sketch

Rather than filling the Strategy Sketch with words, you can also draw it in pictures. This visualization shows the overall structure and story of your strategy in a more inspiring and fun way than just in text. This type of visualization is great for stimulating creativity during the strategy generation process and for sharing the strategy with others.

**Comcom's strategy**

## Causal map or mind map

A causal map shows the causal logic of how you achieve your goals and how different parts of your strategy causally link together. At the top of the map draw high-level goals, and below that draw sub-goals and what is needed to achieve them. A mind map is similar, but it puts high-level goals at the center instead of the top. Around that you put the sub-goals etc. This visualization is great for achieving coherence in your strategy and for turning it into actionable plans. To make a causal map or mindmap start with putting the core of your strategy at the top and then connect it to all the other elements in such a way that the causal logic becomes clear.

# Step 5

## Strategy roadmap

A roadmap visualizes how your strategy unfolds over time. It presents the major developments in the environment and shows how you build up your strategy along with these developments. As a high-level visualization of your strategy over time, a roadmap is a good starting point for making a project plan or a Gantt chart. The most straightforward way to create a roadmap is to divide the 'road' towards realizing your new strategy into a couple of phases and plot these horizontally on a sheet of paper. Then, vertically select a number of key factors that change over time. For this you can select a few or even all of the ten elements of the Strategy Sketch. In this way you can show, for example, how you build up your resources and competences over time, which customers and needs you serve over time, and so on.

### Macman's strategy

| Element | Year 1 | Year 2 | Year 3 |
|---|---|---|---|
| Value proposition | Add personalized services | Offer small complementary equipment | Start offering machine types X and Z |
| Resources & competences | Train engineers to sell additional services to customers | Expand our plant, buy equipment, hire additional engineers | |
| Partners | | Get an additional steel supplier | |
| Revenue model | Aim: 80% of income from selling current machines, 20% from services | Aim: 60% from current machines, 30% services, 10% new machines | Aim: 40% current machines, 30% services, 30% new machines |
| Organizational climate | Maintain our hard-working and loyal culture. Increase the entrepreneurial spirit and capabilities | | |
| And so on | ... | And so on | ... |

# Pitching your strategy

Maybe you have seen the TV program Dragon's Den. On this program entrepreneurs have a few minutes to pitch their business ideas to a panel of potential investors. If they can convince one or more investors of the viability of their venture, they can get funding and immediately start negotiating about this. There's a big chance there will be a point when you also have to pitch your strategy. This is not necessarily a formal pitch to investors. It can also be a quick explanation to a customer or a brief moment when you need to convince someone of your strategy. For those occasions you can use the following steps and guidelines to make sure that you deliver a convincing strategy pitch.

## "There's a big chance that there will be a point when you have to pitch your strategy to someone."

### Step 1 Choose the right moment to pitch

An important decision is when to pitch your strategy. You can be too early, for example, when you're not yet able to answer some basic questions about the strategy. But you can also be too late, especially if you want feedback or need to keep the people you pitch to involved in the strategy generation process. The right time to pitch will depend on the reasons you are pitching. If you're pitching for feedback this can be early in the strategy development process. But if you need to convince a potential investor, it should be as crystalized as possible. Maybe you cannot schedule the pitch yourself, but a date is given to you. In that case you have a clear deadline and you know when you need to be ready to pitch.

### Step 2 Know who to pitch to

A second step is to be clearly aware of the people you are pitching to. You want to know their goals and interests and understand how the new strategy can help them personally. Also, you should know what you want from them, and thus why you are pitching your strategy to them. Possible panels include:

183

- An informal 'friendly' panel of critical insiders and/or outsiders. This is the safest kind of panel you can pitch to. It is mainly meant to further improve the strategy or as a test run for a more formal pitch later in the process. Therefore, unlike in the other pitches you may want to show unresolved problems or ask targeted questions so that you get the feedback that you need.
- The board of directors of your organization. Maybe you are part of a strategy team or business development team that is concerned with developing a new strategy. To continue with the strategy you may first need the support, approval, or resources from the board of the organization. This pitch is more formal than the previous one and should be more convincing.
- One or more potential investors such as venture capitalists, business angels, banks, or other investment funds. In this case, there should be no problems or lack of clarity anymore and the pitch should be as convincing as possible. You should make sure that you are pitching to the right kind of investors (for example, do they invest in the kind of organizations that you are?) and that you know whether they want to maximize their profits (such as venture capitalists) or get their money back (banks).

## Step 3 — Prepare and deliver the pitch

The third and main step is to turn the strategy that you have developed into a convincing pitch. In addition to what you have already seen in this chapter about how to formulate your strategy, it is useful to include the following elements in your pitch:

1. What the product, service, or strategy is and how it is unique. It is fatal for a pitch if people don't understand what you are intending.

2. What it does for your audience. You should show how the strategy helps the people you are pitching to (see also Step 2 above).

3. Who you are and why you will be successful. Especially if pitching to people outside the organization you want to show the strengths of your organization or team so that your audience believes that you can do it.

4. What you want from your audience. Your pitch is not a pitch for the sake of pitching. You want something and you should clearly express that. For example, be clear about whether you want them to make an investment, give approval, or provide feedback.

# "A strategy pitch is just as much or even more about you than about the strategy itself."

When preparing and delivering the pitch it is furthermore useful to pay attention to the following guidelines:

- **See it their way and sell to them.** Put yourself in their shoes and think about what would convince you. Don't do a neutral pitch that could have been given anywhere (you might use the Empathy map for this that we saw on page 72).
- **Create excitement.** Strategy seems something primarily rational, but that is a misconception. Many crucial strategic decisions are made based on emotions. Therefore make sure you excite your audience.
- **Be honest and stay grounded.** Don't exaggerate and certainly don't lie. Modesty often works more convincingly, and don't think you can fool your audience.
- **Use facts and figures.** Although market research might not give you the kind of certainty that you want as a basis for your strategy, the facts and figures that it produces work very convincingly. Use this.
- **You are also presenting yourself.** A strategy pitch is just as much or even more about you than about the strategy itself. You are part of the package, and your audience judges whether they believe you can make the strategy happen.
- **Learn and persist.** It is unlikely that you will get a standing ovation for your pitch. You will probably get critical comments, rejections, and the like. Politely thank your audience and improve your strategy and your next pitch.
- **Use your time wisely.** You probably have a fixed amount of time that you can use. Don't pitch for any longer, and if you're running out of time, select what you still want to say rather than speaking faster.

Once you've done all of this you've done everything you can to generate a good strategy. This is of course no guarantee that it will also work out as expected. However, you have significantly increased your chances.

# 8 Strategy generation formats

After having gone through the previous chapters you have all the necessary ingredients for strategy generation. You now know about the five steps of the strategy generation process and you have checklists, questions, examples, exercises, and models to support each step. With all of this you should be able to successfully generate new strategy for your organization.

So, you're basically done. However, in this last chapter I want to share with you a number formats that you could use to perform the five steps on your own or with a group of people. Maybe you already have your own way of working, and maybe you have even already started while going through this book. In that case, you can skip this chapter and just go on. If, on the other hand, you're still looking for a way to apply the five steps, or if you want to see some varieties, this chapter can be useful for you.

> ### Strategy generation formats:
> Different forms of interaction used to perform strategy generation processes.

One format you have already seen on page 111: The fast and frugal format. Based on just Chapter 4, that format guided you in a rather quick way through the strategy generation process. In this chapter you will find five additional formats. The point of presenting these is not that you should necessarily choose between them. Rather, they are meant to show the breadth of possible formats and to inspire you. The formats are:

1. Do-it-yourself
2. Nominal group technique (Post-it™ sessions)
3. Breakout groups
4. Brainwriting
5. Phase-gate approach

# Format 1: Do-it-yourself

The most straightforward way to go through the strategy generation process is to do every step on your own. This simply means that you follow the guidelines of Chapters 4-7 and map, assess, innovate, and formulate your strategy along the way – maybe that's even what you did while reading the book. While this could generally work well, you will miss out the diversity and dynamics that you would have had if you had a team to work with. The main trick in this format then is to *simulate* diversity and dynamics so that you have a sufficiently rich process that is not limited by the way of thinking of a single person. While you are on your own, you can do various things to create diversity and dynamics:

1 **Use this book.** This entire book compensates for the lack of a team to work with. Especially when you are on your own, the various tools, questions, and checklists foster divergent thinking so that you look further than you would normally do.

2 **Take breaks.** It also helps to intentionally schedule breaks throughout the process. The reason is that these help you to subconsciously process all the information so that it can support your conscious activities. A break can be a night of sleep, but also another activity that requires mental effort such as reading a difficult book or solving a challenging problem. Research has shown that the latter leads to better decisions than just taking a rest.

3 **Move.** Yet another trick to create 'different you's' is to change contexts during the strategy generation process. Different places cause different moods, and they can give you different sources of inspiration. This is particularly useful during the innovation step. For me, for example, traveling by train or plane, or being in coffee places in different cities works well.

4 **Get feedback.** Of course this means you are not doing it all by yourself anymore. But you should always take the opportunity to share your ideas with others to get feedback. One way that works well is using a regular sparring partner with whom you can discuss your progress. If you cannot do that or don't want to, you should still talk with other people because it is indispensable for good strategy generation.

## "If you do it all by yourself, the main trick is to simulate diversity and dynamics."

## Format 2: Nominal group technique (or Post-it™ session)

The nominal group technique is a well-known and widely used technique for all kinds of decision-making, problem solving, and solution generation processes with a group. Maybe you know it better as a Post-it session. It seems quite trendy nowadays to bash this technique and to argue that it just leads to a big pile of Post-it notes but to no real effect. This is nonsense. These critiques just show that this technique has not been used properly or not for the right reason. If, on the other hand, you structure it well (by using for example the Strategy Sketch) and make sure you also pay attention to how you narrow down the ideas that are generated, this can still be a very effective format. When adapted to strategy generation it looks as follows:

1 Get a group of people together that are quite different and relevant for your strategy. This can be the management team or board, but you can involve others as well, including employees, customers, or suppliers.

2 Print or draw the Strategy Sketch on a large sheet of paper. At least DIN A3 or Tabloid format, but larger is better (DIN A0 or E-size). Put it on a table or wall so that everyone can see it.

3   Map out the existing strategy. Let everyone write his or her contributions on individual Post-it notes. This works best if you start doing this element by element (as argued previously, I usually start with resources and competences). You can encourage people by asking the first set of 'Questions to ask' for each element. When I do this, I usually get things that people find good about their current strategy and things that are not so good or that they would still need. To mark the difference, I ask them to use green notes for the first and orange notes for the latter.

4   Collect the notes and stick them on the Strategy Sketch. While doing this, everyone can respond and write additional notes. Don't worry if this part of the process gets a bit messy. It doesn't really matter if people don't follow the particular order of elements that you have in mind. To keep the flow right, you should allow them to write down anything they want. But you should make sure you put the notes in the right place on the Strategy Sketch.

## "Don't worry if this part of the process gets a bit messy."

5   Now you can go down two paths:

A   Assess the strategy, for example by asking everyone to choose the three most important strengths of the current strategy – per element or for the strategy as a whole. A simple way to do this is to give everyone three small stickers that they can stick on what they think are the key strengths. After this procedure you can discuss and come to an agreement about what the key strengths of the current strategy are. These form a solid basis for the new strategy. Subsequently you start innovating by using the approach explained under 'b' below.

B   Instead of assessing first, you start innovating the strategy by applying one or more of the innovation approaches from Chapter 6. To do this again use the Post-it notes approach, preferably using a different color so that you can still distinguish between what you already have and what is new

(I usually use yellow notes for this). You can stimulate ideas by sharing the second set of 'Questions to ask' per element and the 'Inspirational checklists'. After that you can assess the ideas in a similar way as for 5a.

6 After step 5 you may have multiple ideas for a new strategy. You probably cannot execute all of them, and they are probably still fragments that need to be turned into a coherent strategy. To do this, pick the three most promising ideas (for example using the same procedure as under 5a, or a more systematic assessment based on Chapter 5) and develop them further on separate empty Strategy Sketches.

7 Decide which strategy is the best for your organization. Then formulate its core and structure in words and/or pictures (see previous chapter).

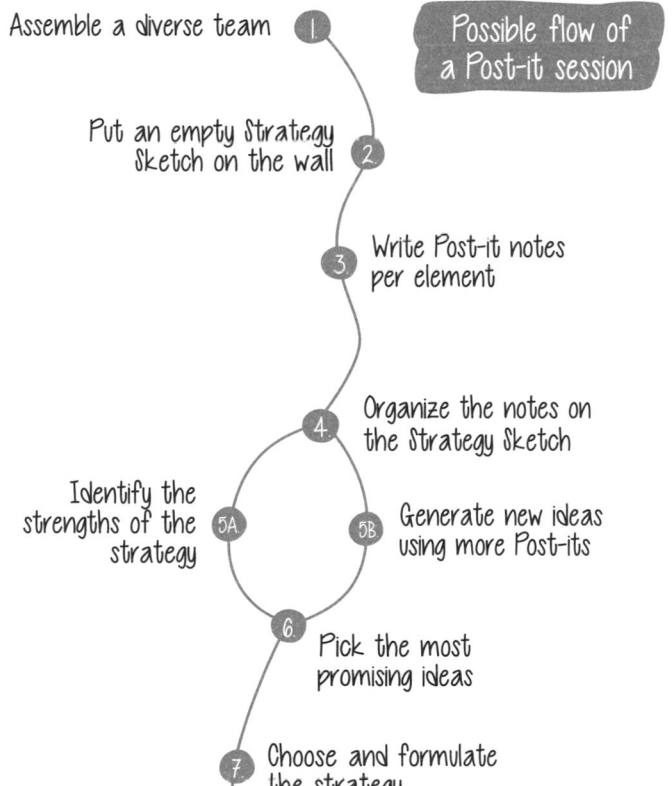

Assemble a diverse team — 1

Possible flow of a Post-it session

Put an empty Strategy Sketch on the wall — 2

3 — Write Post-it notes per element

4 — Organize the notes on the Strategy Sketch

Identify the strengths of the strategy — 5A

5B — Generate new ideas using more Post-its

6 — Pick the most promising ideas

7 — Choose and formulate the strategy

# Format 3: Breakout groups

The basic procedure for breakout groups is similar to the nominal group technique. You also gather a group of people; use the Strategy Sketch to map the strategy, assess it, innovate it, and formulate it in a way so that it can be communicated. Yet, instead of doing the entire session with the whole group, you break it down into smaller groups or pairs. This works particularly well in steps 3, 5b, and 6:

- In **step 3**, you could break out in order to get different descriptions of the current strategy. This works particularly well if you have different groups of people involved which might have different views on the strategy, such as groups of managers and employees.
- You could also choose to do wait until **step 5** until you use breakout groups. In this way you start with a common understanding of the current strategy, after which idea generation takes place in different groups.
- Breakout groups also work well in **step 6**. In that case strategy generation, assessment, and some innovation all take place with the whole group, but the further development of ideas into separate strategies takes place in the breakout groups.

When you use this format, make sure you have multiple copies of the Strategy Sketch available that people can use in the breakout groups. DIN A3 / Tabloid or DIN A2 / C-size format is generally sufficient.

# Format 4: Brainwriting

A fourth format for strategy generation is brainwriting. The main difference from the nominal group technique is that most communication during this process takes place in written form. The basic approach with brainwriting is that each team member starts by writing something down on a sheet of paper and after a couple of minutes passes it on to the next person. The next person adds his or her ideas, and after a couple of minutes passes it on to the next, and so on. In this way after several rounds everyone has contributed to every piece of paper.

Compared to brainstorming, brainwriting is less dynamic. However, it increases the likelihood of getting contributions from less talkative or introverted people. Furthermore, brainwriting is less sensitive to groupthink, thereby avoiding a too early consensus. Brainwriting can be used for Steps 2-5 of the strategy generation process.

"Brainwriting increases the likelihood of getting contributions from less talkative or introverted people and it is less sensitive to groupthink."

### For mapping strategy

This works ideally if you have a team of 5 or 10. Use one sheet of paper for each element of the Strategy Sketch. With a team of 10, let everyone start with one of these sheets and put their ideas for that element on the sheet of paper. After a couple of minutes the sheets are passed onto the next person and so on. After 10 rounds everyone has contributed to every element of the Strategy Sketch. With a team of 5 you let everyone start with two elements and for other team sizes you have to be a bit creative. If there are elements more important to your organization, you might, for example, have two people starting with those elements.

### For assessing strategy

When using brainwriting for strategy assessment, it is important that there is a clear understanding of what is being assessed. This can, for example, be a completed Strategy Sketch, a summary of the strategy, or a particular element of the strategy. In this case use one sheet per strategy check. Let everyone start with applying a different strategy check by writing down the main strengths and weaknesses of the strategy from the perspective of that check. Then, the sheets are passed onto the next person until everyone has applied all the checks.

### For innovating strategy

For innovating strategy different starting points are possible, depending on which innovation approach you choose you can do brainwriting as follows:

- **Elementary innovation:** Use one sheet per element of the Strategy Sketch and let everyone come up with new ideas for that element one after another.
- **Amplifying innovation:** Use one sheet per scalability tactic and pass them on so that everyone contributes to every tactic.
- **Routed Innovation:** Use one sheet per innovation route and have everyone contribute one after another.
- **Projective innovation:** Use one sheet per identified trend or uncertainty and circulate so that everyone thinks about the possible implications of each trend and uncertainty.
- **Freestyle innovation:** Use one 'What if...' scenario per sheet and let everyone contribute their ideas by passing on the sheets.

### For formulating strategy

Finally, brainwriting is also suitable for formulating your strategy. To do this you could ask everyone to start with a different core (one of the ten elements, see the previous chapter), complete the first one or two sentences and hand it to the next person after a couple of minutes. The next person adds the next one or two sentences and after several rounds you have formulated a set of complete strategies. At the end, the team can choose the best one, for example by using the sticker procedure of the nominal group technique.

# Format 5: Phase-gate approach

The final and most extensive format is the phase-gate (or stage-gate or traffic-light) approach to strategy generation. The main idea of this format is that you divide the strategy generation process into a number of clear phases separated by 'gates' (or traffic lights). At each gate, a decision is made about whether and how to continue the strategy generation process.

There are various ways to divide the process into phases. Your organization might be used to working with particular phases, such as those of the Stage-Gate® innovation process or project management techniques such as PRINCE2®. In that case it makes sense to use similar phases for strategy generation. If, on the other hand, you feel free in deciding which phases to use you could consider the following five:

# "For less risky strategies it is recommended to use a simpler approach with fewer phases and early piloting."

1  **Idea phase:** The first phase is the generation of an idea that could serve as the basis for a new strategy generation process. This can be based on any strategy element such as a new way to use resources, an unmet customer need, or an emerging opportunity.

As a *gate* for this phase you can use a 2-minute 'soap-box' pitch or a half-page description that can be assessed by the board or other relevant persons. The result is a 'go' (continue, green light), a 'go back' (revise, amber light), or a 'no go' (stop, red light).

2  **Sketch phase:** The next phase is turning the idea into a complete strategy by filling out all elements of the Strategy Sketch using the steps of the strategy generation process.

As a *gate* for this phase you can use the strategy pitch presented on page 183 or a 4-5 page document with a convincing explanation of the strategy. Again a 'go', 'go back' or 'no go' decision should be taken after this.

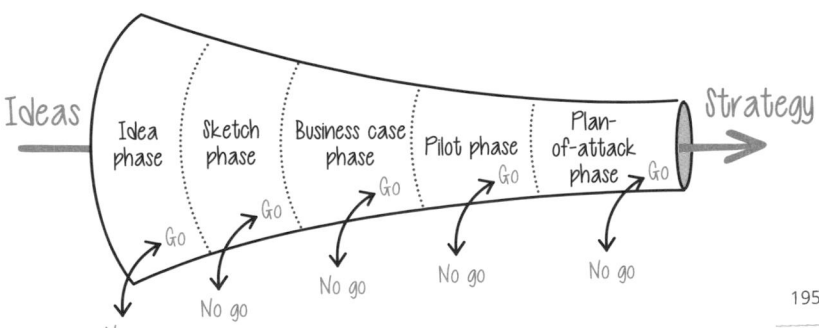

Phase-gate approach to strategy generation

3 **Business case phase:** The third phase is the development of a business case. In this phase you specify what is needed to realize the strategy and calculate whether the expected results will exceed the required investments.

Also, in this phase the *gate* is a decision on the continuation of the process based on a presentation or a written document. As it usually requires some details, you might need at least 10 pages or half an hour (but resist the temptation to write extensive documents).

4 **Pilot phase:** While the first three phases are based on thinking and analysis, the pilot phase is one of actual testing. In this phase you test whether the strategy actually works by rolling it out on a small scale. When you do this, it is important to choose a set of metrics in advance so that you measure the effects systematically.

The 'go' / 'go back' / 'no go' *gate* for this phase should be based on a clear presentation or publication of the findings of the pilot: What has been achieved, what worked, what didn't, etc.

5 **Plan-of-attack phase:** In the fifth phase a final decision on the strategy is made based on an operational plan, or plan-of-attack. This plan should contain the clear next steps that will be made in order to realize the strategy.

The last *gate* is a final 'go' / 'go back' / 'no go' decision on whether to continue with the strategy. This can be based on an extensive strategic plan, but more preferable is a shorter action plan that specifies the main actions to be taken.

With five phases, this is an extensive phase-gate approach. I recommend never making it more complex than that because that would make the strategy generation process over-systematic and bureaucratic without adding any real value. Furthermore, a five-phase approach is only preferred for strategies that require large investments and that are hard or impossible to reverse. For less risky strategies it is generally recommended to use a simpler approach with fewer phases and early piloting. You can, for example, just use phases 1, 2, and 4: You have an idea, turn it into a strategy, and then start piloting. This format reflects a more trial-and-error approach to strategy generation.

# A final recommendation

I wrote this handbook with the aim that it should improve and ease strategy generation for your organization. Based on the idea that strategy generation is a creative, interactive, and emergent process, it proposes a five-step approach to strategy generation supported with a collection of tools and formats. You could of course strictly follow my suggestions, stick to the proposed order of steps, and methodically generate a 'correct' and complete strategy. What I hope and recommend, though, is that you will use this book as a source of insights and inspiration for developing your own personal approach to strategy generation. Only in that way will you be able to truly generate your own unique strategy – your way of sustainable value creation.

"Use this book as a source of insights and inspiration for developing your own approach to strategy generation."

# Afterword

We're at the end of the book now and there is not much more to say. I've done my best to put all that I have experienced about strategy in the past years together in a practical handbook that, I hope, helps you in improving your strategy and making it work.

A book is rather fixed once printed. As a reader/user you can add your own notes, turning this into your own personal handbook, but I cannot add or change anything more before the next print. However, on the accompanying website (www.thestrategyhandbook.com) you will find some further tools and information – including a printable version of the Strategy Sketch.

## A word of thanks

I could never have written this book on my own. Over the past few years I have discussed ideas, texts, chapters, and models with numerous entrepreneurs, experts, managers, directors, academics, students, friends, and the like. Some of them were my clients, others were participants at my strategy and entrepreneurship courses at the University of Twente, VentureLab International, Amsterdam Business School, and TSM business school, and still others participated in various seminars, workshops, and conversations. It would go to far to name all of them personally – if only because I am absent-minded enough to be 100% sure I would forget some of them. However, if you are one of them, thank you so much! (and also my apologies for knowingly and unknowingly letting you be a guinea pig...)

There are a few people I want to thank personally though, since they took the effort to read through the drafts of this book and comment on it. Stuart, thank you for confronting me with the lacking personality of earlier versions of the book and your extremely fast and to-the-point feedback. Jeroen, thank you for comparing the book to other books and pointing out its underdeveloped normative message. JC, thank you for your ever critical and unconventional view on strategy and for sharpening me up in the journey towards this book. Martin, thank you for your enthusiasm and for sharing with me your approach to strategy and innovation. Jason, thank you for your detailed comments and for also pointing out the parts you particularly liked. Björn, thank you for your precision and for contrasting the book with the business model literature. Hidde, thank you for your critical view and constructive suggestions. Saras, thank you for inspiring me with your work on effectuation and for bringing in the idea of exercises. And finally, Caroline, thank you for reading the entire book word for word, for telling me where it was boring, superfluous, or incomprehensible, for supporting me with everything else that made it possible to write this book, and for being my wife.

I am grateful to all of you and really appreciate that you've bothered to help me in writing this book. Your contributions have made it a much better book than it was. Any remaining ambiguities or errors are mine.

Although this book has reached its final page, it is definitely not the end of my writing efforts. There's more than one other book that I want to write and that I hope to share with you in the not-so-distant future. As a next step, my journey now continues with Part 2 of this book: Strategy Execution.

Happy strategizing!


Jeroen Kraaijenbrink

*www.thestrategyhandbook.com*
*@JKraaijenbrink*